TEN ANCHORS

TEN ANCHORS

For Navigating the Sea of life
A Primer for Young Catholics

Reflections on ten dimensions of the Christian Faith that are at the heart of the Roman Catholic experience. Written with young Catholics in mind, Catholics of all ages will find these reflections helpful in living the Catholic tradidion today.

JOHN E. FORLITI

First published in 2010.
This edition published in 2013 with minor edits and new format.

ISBN 918-0-557-59022-3

Printed by PEAK Printing, Saint Paul Minnesota
Updated layout and design by Stephanie Forliti, White Bear Lake Minnesota

The anchor, a symbol found in early Christian art, means hope. The stock on top of the anchor made the anchor resemble a cross. Thus, for early Christians, an anchor meant hope in the Cross of Christ Jesus. Another symbol found in early Christian art is the ship, often depicted with St. Peter at the helm steering the Church through stormy and rough waters. In Catholic tradition the church is referred to as "the Barque of Peter." Anchors were used to keep the ship steady in the midst of challenging times.

ACKNOWLEDGEMENTS

My thanks to the host of readers who've reviewed various versions of the developing manuscript.

Listed in no particular order, they are:
Mark Alt, Molly Story, Matt Chaffin, Bryan Linehan, Ann Deuvel, Michelle Fischer,
Geoffry Ludvik, Maggie Malone-Pavolney, Richard Engler, Mike Powers,
Jack Kreitzer, Nancy Scanlan, Mal Scanlan, Lou Anne Tighe, Dave Berrisford,
Tom Haider, Fr. Steve Adrian, Frank Miley, Kathy Miley, Mike Fitzgerald,
Fr. Ken LaVan, Bev Quintavalle, Joanne Hense-Honsa, Peter Honsa.

Special thanks to Amy Forliti for her editing skills,
and to Jason Fuglsby for his computer assistance.

Table of Contents

INTRODUCTION

If, at times, you feel afloat, drifting, wondering where you might land next, worried about surviving the next storm, you might consider tying your life to an anchor.

When, at other times, the sea is calm, you might double check to be sure the anchors are on board and at the ready. You never know.

The teen and young adult years can be among the most challenging in the faith journey of a young Catholic. This is the time when many make life long choices about personal identity, belief in God, religious affiliation, friendships, and careers. It is also the time when youth are hit hard by various media hoping to win their dollars and loyalty to name brands. And it is the time when youth are most vulnerable and likely to make unwise choices about alcohol, drugs, sex, friendships, e-media, and religion.

This book is offered to young Catholics to help them reflect on one of the most precious gifts they received at their baptism, namely, membership in the Roman Catholic Church. It is all too easy to miss the message in a culture that is highly sexualized and secular, and dominated by a media that feels free to take a whack at the Church and religion in general. Making it easier to miss the message are the failures of the Church in dealing with the weakness and scandals of some of its leaders.

So, it may be the worst of times to be a person of faith, but it may also be the best of times. Having lived through both, I believe young Catholics today want the best for themselves and for their children as they prepare for leadership in the 21st century. A culture is as strong as its institutions are healthy. If our nation is to be a beacon of justice for the oppressed and the poor, a participant in healing some of the hurt around the globe, and a peacemaker at home and abroad, our institutions must be strong. All of them: politics, medicine, business, education, the judiciary, social welfare, and religion, to name some of the most obvious. For this to happen, society needs to raise up leaders in every field who have the highest levels of moral integrity, and a strong desire to serve the common good.

In its two thousand year history, the Catholic Church has done it all, both the best and the worst. While others may choose to write about its failures, this book will focus on its successes. The Catholic Church has been and will continue to be a force for good in the world. Future generations will be blessed by the Catholic youth of today who choose to embrace their Baptismal calling and live their faith to the fullest with enthusiasm and zeal. As with our other institutions, all of which serve as the backbone of society, our Church needs dedicated and talented leaders and members whose faith is strong and active.

Divided into ten major themes, this book can serve as a resource for personal growth, both for the individual Catholic and the community of faith at large. Take your time to read and ponder. Let the treasures of your faith speak to your heart as well as your head. Jesus invites you to embrace Him as the Way, the Truth, and the Life. Each chapter concludes with a starter list of Catholic practice, values and actions that can support and nourish your faith, which will build a stronger Church, which, in turn, will result in a stronger society and more peaceful world. Know that your commitment and efforts to activate your faith will be effective in transforming the world.

My dad loved to take us fishing. My job oftentimes was to sit in the front of the boat and drop the anchor whenever he said. Usually the anchor would hold and we would stay in the same spot until we pulled anchor and headed for another spot.

Sometimes the anchor would not hold. Either the rope joining the anchor to the boat was too short, unable to lodge into the lake bottom tight enough to hold us, or the wind was too strong and the anchor not heavy enough to beat the wind, or the anchor was built too smoothly and couldn't attach itself to something that might hold until we pulled anchor and moved on.

Anchors are good to have, especially anchors you can count on. You do not want to drift too far from your purpose in life.

Faith is an anchor. That is what this book is about.

Allow me to share some stories about the anchors in my life. My hope is that in some small way my stories may speak to your life. But first, a bit about faith and its relationship to trust.

What is Faith?

Faith is the choice people make to believe someone or something. It is what we do when we are dealing with human experiences which either can't be proven or which fall into an area that reason doesn't reach. For example, science is very good at discovering facts about our universe, our planet earth and much of what is in and on this global home of ours. Science is good at telling us the what and how of things, but not the who and why. The who and why are matters of faith. Who made the universe and why, only faith can answer.

Faith comes in various sizes. Blind faith is a huge act of faith, to take something strictly on the basis of another's word, or simply to choose to believe someone or something without any evidence at all. Blind faith can be totally foolish, even irrational or dangerous. If someone tells you that there is a soft mattress beneath the cliff's edge and you won't get hurt if you jump, your trust is at stake. If you are a child and your trusted dad is the one telling you to jump, your belief may be blind but not foolish. If an enemy is the tempter, however, you will wisely check it out first! And then probably not jump anyway.

Faith always involves some unknowns, some degree of uncertainty, some level of doubt. For example, if we knew for certain that the mattress was beneath the cliff, we would not need faith.

When science does not answer certain questions about our universe we either choose to dodge the question or make an act of faith about them. A prime example: I cannot prove that God exists and that it was God who made the universe. But, judging from what I see and experience, I choose to believe that a Creator God made everything and that this God has to be beautiful, powerful, personal, intelligent, beyond my imagination, beyond my comprehension. I have thought about but rejected the idea that it all happened on its own or accidentally. No other explanation makes sense except that there is a God. I am a believer. For me and billions of other people, belief in God is a totally reasonable and rational choice.

So, is the atheist also a believer? Yes. An atheist cannot prove that God does not exist so he or she makes an act of faith that God does not exist. Some would argue that this position is even less rational than the choice for belief in God's existence.

Welcome to the world of belief! Faith is a normal part of everyday life. We get up in the morning, most mornings anyway, believing that life is worth living, and that the day will move along okay. We can't prove it, but we believe it. If we have a bit of evidence that the day will be a good one –we've got the day off, going to pick up the lottery winnings, spending time with a best friend,-- we walk into the day confident. (The word confident has its roots in two Latin words *con fide*, which means **with faith**).

Since faith says YES in spite of the darkness, confidence in ourselves making it through the day successfully always helps. Faith has power. A high school athlete's or an actor's self-confidence on stage can make all the difference in the world on how well he or she performs.

Faith and Trust

Faith and trust are twins. They go together. When we have faith in someone or something, we are placing our trust in that person or thing. Everyone makes acts of faith every day. When we get up in the morning we trust that the day will go okay. Should we wake up with a blistering ache somewhere in our body we probably won't trust in that day being a good one but our trust shifts to believing that we will get through it in spite of the pain.

Typically, if you and I are like most people, our acts of faith and trust do not have to be consciously made. Most hours of most days we operate on auto pilot. In the middle of the night we trust that daylight will come. We trust the electric power company as we plug in our toasters. We trust the bus driver as we drop the fare into the box. We trust in the smile of a friend, the welcome of a teacher, the greeting of our parents, the value of our lunch money. Faith and trust are part of everyday life.

Which means that doubt is also a part of everyday life. Doubt plays a significant role in faith. Facing up to our doubts is what makes faith stronger. Every time I have questioned a proposition of faith I have had to make a decision about it. I could say No to the existence of God, or to Jesus as my Redeemer and choose not to believe. But whenever I have reconsidered these two beliefs, I have said Yes with even greater affirmation. Thus, doubt became a means to a stronger faith.

So, why can it be so hard to have faith in God, faith in Jesus, faith in the Church? For one thing, God can be so difficult to see, impossible to imagine, and often distant emotionally. I can talk to God, out loud, and before I know it, the medics in white coats appear to haul me off to the psych ward. (Not really, but we can feel foolish when we realize we might just be talking to ourselves.)

Have you ever tried to imagine what God looks like? I tried air. I tried ghost. I tried breath. I tried spirit. I tried to imagine **NOTHING**, in capitals! Try it and see what you come up with! It can't be done. God cannot be seen by human eyes. So, you might conclude, if God can't be seen, God does not exist. Well, that argument doesn't get me anywhere. I can't see the air I am breathing but I am certain it exists. I can't see hope or faith or courage or honesty but I know when they are present or are lacking.

I know God exists because I can see *the evidence*. Every aspect in the natural world, from the tiniest creature to the expansive galaxies, is evidence of the divine imagination, incredible power and might, and a generous love. Look around, look within. The love of God is manifest. For Christians, God's love is blatantly evident in the life, passion, death, and resurrection of Jesus Christ. To know Him is to love Him and to love as He loved.

The earliest disciples of Jesus were recognized for their care for one another. Tertullian, a first century Christian author wrote: "See these Christians, how they love one another." So, we begin with a look at Anchor #1, Compassion.

ANCHOR ONE
Compassion

The first Christians took up collections for the poor,
for widows and children. Since then numerous religious
congregations have been founded to deliver the compassion of
Jesus to the sick and dying, the marginalized and oppressed.
Compassion is our middle name, individually and collectively.

FROM MOVEMENT TO INSTITUTION

As a young Catholic you can be proud of your Church for many reasons, not least of which is how it has, and continues to, respond to human needs. Beginning with the very first followers of Jesus, Christians have come to the aid of those in need.

> *"Now the company of those who believed were of one heart and soul, and no one said that any of the things that he possessed was his own, but they had everything in common. And with great power the apostles gave their testimony to the resurrection of the Lord Jesus and great grace was upon them all. There was not a needy person among them, for as many as were in possession of lands or houses, sold them and brought the proceeds of what was sold and laid it at the apostles' feet and distribution was made to each as any had need."*
>
> *(Acts of the Apostles, 4: 32-35)*

Christianity began as a movement. As with all movements that last, this movement of followers of Jesus developed into an institution. The beautiful thing about institutions is that they have staying power while movements tend to be temporary. A recent example of this in the United States is the Civil Rights movement led by Dr. Martin Luther King, Jr. There was a serious human need. Leaders emerged with a passionate desire to respond to the need. More and more people joined in, and the movement spread. As any movement grows, it tends to develop clarity in its mission, its goals, its policies and procedures. When that happens, it becomes institutionalized, as it formalizes its identity and purpose in a charter or constitution, establishes clear expectations for its membership, and issues guidelines and regulations.

Movements evolving into institutions have both positive and negative aspects. On the positive side, institutions provide a certain stability and endurance while movements, by their very nature, are more spontaneous and fluid. On the negative side, institutions can become stale and stiff, lacking passion and vitality which are characteristic of movements. But, an important contribution of institutions is that their very stability serves as the breeding ground for new movements.

The Catholic Church, as one of the oldest institutions in existence, has a history filled with the birth of movements evolving into institutions. And within many of these institutions, some of which are more than fifteen hundred years old (e.g. the Benedictine Orders which operate, among others, St. John's University and College of St. Benedict near St. Cloud, Minnesota) other movements developed. Religious Orders all had their origins with individuals who felt drawn to respond to a particular need, attracted others to join them, and offered a fresh face for the Gospel.

BENEDICT AND SCHOLASTICA

Benedict and Scholastica were siblings who, in the sixth century, began a string of separate monastic foundations for men and women. Directed by the Rule that Benedict developed, monasteries spread throughout Europe, numbering into the hundreds by the 12th century. Today, located around the globe, Benedictine communities operate schools and parishes while maintaining their special charism of *Ora et Labora*, prayer and work for their members with the "Benedictine tradition" of welcoming travelers and strangers as Christ himself.

FRANCIS AND CLARE

Francis (+ 1226) and Clare (+ 1253) of Assisi started a movement eight centuries ago which continues today to give witness worldwide to simplicity of life and service to the poor. Franciscans of many variations run hospitals, schools, food shelves, homes for AIDS patients, retreat centers and other ministries.

IGNATIUS LOYOLA

Ignatius Loyola (+ 1556) founded the Jesuit Order of men whose worldwide presence provides education from elementary to graduate education. Ignatian spirituality is their foundation with justice issues given high priority, particularly in the areas of war and peace, immigration, poverty, service to refugees, and relief services.

JANE DE CHANTAL

Jane De Chantal (+ 1641) founded the Visitation Sisters. At Visitation Convent school in St. Paul the Sisters have taught girls for more than a century, and in recent years have established a courageous ministry of a peaceful presence in one of the Twin Cities most dangerous neighborhoods.

CHARLES LWANGA

Charles Lwanga died a martyr's death in 1887. Forty years later a Religious Order was founded in his name for African men. Currently in Kenya, Uganda, and Tanzania, the Brothers of Charles Lwanga operate elementary, secondary, technical, and college level schools primarily in slum settings.

FRANCES XAVIER CABRINI

Frances Xavier Cabrini (+ 1917) in spite of a lifetime of delicate health, founded 67 institutions (schools, orphanages, nurseries, and hospitals) in her 67 years. Named the patroness of immigrants, Mother Cabrini's special mission was to the Italian immigrants who settled in North and South America. Although afraid of water herself, she crossed the Atlantic more than thirty times, driven by her faith in God and her desire to serve.

TERESA OF CALCUTTA

Teresa of Calcutta, (+ 1997) began her ministry as a teacher then felt called to assist the dying in the streets and slums of Calcutta. Today, in more than 600 missions in 120 countries, some 5,000 Missionaries of Charity serve the poorest of the poor in homes for the dying, refuges for orphaned and abandoned children, treatment centers and hospitals for those suffering from leprosy, and centers for street people, for alcoholics, and for the aged.

These are but a small sampling of the hundreds of congregations of women and men who chose to follow in the footsteps of their founders. Review the history of the Church and you will find heroic women and men, in love with Jesus Christ and the Church, who have sacrificed themselves for the common good of humanity. Such dedication continues today, not only in the parish communities that dot urban, suburban and rural areas worldwide, but also in agencies like Catholic Charities which is organized nationally as well as in local dioceses. Add to these official resources the many other Catholic groups whose purpose is to lessen the effects of poverty and you have an impressive array of followers of Jesus doing incalculable good work for millions of recipients. More on Catholic Charities later, but first a look at a movement which has tended to resist institutionalization, the Catholic Worker movement founded by Dorothy Day.

DOROTHY DAY lived a very interesting and unusual life. Born into an Episcopalian family, as a child she lost interest in religion and as a young adult began to associate with radical socialist causes. Once jailed for picketing the White House she later got involved in a relationship that led to an abortion, a decision she regretted the rest of her life. A bit older and wiser, she fell deeply in love with another man, gave birth to a daughter whom she raised, but lost her lover who would not accept her decision to join the Catholic Church. During some of her most difficult times Dorothy would seek peace and consolation in a Catholic church near her apartment. While her comrades freely criticized the Church for its power and wealth, she chose to see another side, namely, the Church of the masses of people, of immigrants, of care for the poorest of the poor. She also began to cherish the Church's "sense of life in its wholeness and holiness, of transcendence, order, and obedience." (Ellsberg, Robert. *By Little and By Little*, Selected writings of Dorothy Day, page xxii).

Dorothy Day died in 1980, at the age of eighty-five. I was moved by her visit with us seminarians shortly before I was ordained. She had a gentle presence, with an exceptional story of disappointment, hard work, and genuine love of God. Her Catholic faith was her daily companion and dependable anchor in life. Her spiritual legacy includes The Catholic Worker, a newspaper she first published in 1933. It became her means of challenging injustices, war, the status quo, and limpid faith. Her spirituality was deeply rooted in Jesus and His Gospel, manifested primarily by sacrifice, worship, and a sense of reverence.

This woman inspired a movement which quickly gave birth to Houses of Hospitality across the U.S., operated by Catholic Worker communities which were characterized "by a spirit of functional anarchy, an abhorrence of regulations, and a basic tolerance of persons of all backgrounds. (Ellsberg, p. xxix.) She was truly a unique expression of God's love for every human being and for all creation. In her search for God, Dorothy Day discovered a rich vein of spiritual vitality in the deepest recesses of the institutional Church. Her legacy continues to inspire people of all faiths to care for the earth and for people in need.

Most, if not all, Catholic dioceses around the world have formal and effective organizations that deliver much needed services to people in need. For U.S. Catholics, the agency and programs that accomplish these services is Catholic Charities.

CATHOLIC CHARITIES USA is the national office for over 1,700 local Catholic Charities agencies and programs nationwide. Catholic Charities USA provides strong leadership and support to enhance the work of local diocesan agencies in their efforts to *reduce poverty, support families, and empower communities*. Catholic Charities USA's members provide help and create hope for more than 8.5 million people of all faiths each year. It was founded in 1910 on the campus of Catholic University of America in Washington, DC, as the National Conference of Catholic Charities.

The Catholic Bishops of the United States established this Conference as their means to promote the establishment of diocesan Catholic Charities bureaus which would encourage the practice of professional social work, bring a sense of solidarity among all those working in charitable ministries, and be the "attorney for the poor." Catholic Charities nationwide is the largest agency serving the poor next to the federal government. In 2009, the budget for Catholic Charities USA was three billion dollars. Catholic Charities USA, with its offices in Washington D.C., also represents the Church in support of legislation that seeks to assist the less fortunate in our country.

Globally, in conjunction with CARITAS INTERNATIONAL, Catholic Charities USA works with other Catholic agencies from around the world when disasters occur and massive relief efforts are required. Caritas International is the global network of Catholic charitable and relief agencies. In recent years, it provided immediate and critical aid to victims of the tsunami that hit Samoa, earthquakes that struck Indonesia, Italy, and Haiti, and the massive migration of peoples at Darfur and other war-torn regions. Catholic agencies, through the networking of Caritas International, are the fourth largest provider of assistance in the HIV AIDS crisis in Africa. It is one of the largest relief efforts by any church or organization in the world.

To learn more about what local diocesan Charities agencies can do, let's take a look at one of them, CATHOLIC CHARITIES FOR THE ARCHDIOCESE OF ST. PAUL AND MINNEAPOLIS. This agency serves the homeless by providing housing, food, clothing and shelter; its programs assist families in adopting children, offer special support to fathers of families, help the unemployed find work, assist refugees with employment and housing; provide counseling to divorced and separated, provide a home for boys, a home for inebriates, and safe housing for the working poor. Their budget in 2009 was thirty-six million dollars, monies coming from various sources including government grants, fund-raising events, and support from the local Catholic community, primarily through the 200 plus parishes in the Twin Cities and surrounding area. The number of people served in 2009 alone through its forty programs was 35,000.

Two of its most visible programs in the Twin Cities are the Dorothy Day Center in St. Paul and the Exodus Hotel in Minneapolis. The Dorothy Day Center provides meals three times daily for two to three hundred people per meal with the help of hundreds of volunteers (of which I am one) from churches, schools, businesses, and other organizations. When the homeless crisis in downtown Minneapolis became very serious in 1992, St. Olaf Church, the parish I was serving, got involved. They raised 1.2 million dollars to buy an eight story residence next door, and contracted with Catholic Charities to operate a 92 room residence as transitional housing. Known as the Exodus Hotel, it quickly became a national model for assisting men and women to get back on their feet with jobs, rental histories, and renewed hope.

One of the New Movements: Sant' Egidio

A recent movement that had simple beginnings and has now expanded to more than seventy nations is the Community of Sant' Egidio. Named after the abandoned church building that became its first home, the community was begun in Rome by a high school student, Andrea Riccardi, who invited other students like himself to listen to, and put into practice the Gospel of Jesus Christ. The models on which they chose to base their community were the Acts of the Apostles and the life of Francis of Assisi.

I first met members of this community in 1986, and was inspired by what they chose to guide their lives: daily prayer and worship, solidarity with the poor, spread of the Gospel, an open and ecumenical relationship with people of other faiths, and dialogue as a way to peace. Members do not live in communities, and they have their separate careers and work. But they are committed to common prayer daily, and they offer their time and talent to projects of the Community. With 50,000 members in seventy countries, the Community continues to expand.

On one of my visits I was shown three of their most recent projects: a large residence they purchased from contributions of members and was now a dignified home for twenty-four elderly "abandonati" (old folks without families to care for them), a newly furnished nursery for homeless infants with AIDS, and a food center, where meals are prepared and served by members to adults living on the streets. They also have ministries to the mentally disabled, to prisoners, and to the homeless. They look for the marginalized and strive not simply to serve, but also to befriend. I was happy to be asked to sit at the "English-speaking" table at their free lunch center. When they serve meals to the homeless, they strive to have a member of the community (or a visitor like me) at each table to offer hospitality and conversation: food for the spirit as well as for the body!

The next time I was in Rome and visited the Community, they were waiting for leaders from rival factions in Mozambique to arrive for peace talks under their sponsorship. Several agencies had offered to bring the two sides together, but the only group both warring parties trusted was the Community of Sant'Egidio. Their meeting was successful, and the decades long civil war in Mozambique ended.

On this visit I had noticed that the Community had become more organized and structured since its beginning as a movement. I asked one of its founding leaders what they do to keep their efforts going as a movement. His response was memorable: "When a movement becomes institutionalized it is already dead as a movement." That taught me an important lesson. Movements have their own rules, as do institutions. Movements rarely are able to maintain themselves as movements. Their natural development is to develop mission statements, guidelines, constitutions, a historical memory, and formal leadership roles. Many movements, if they do not become institutionalized, disappear.

Though institutions often lack the excitement of movements, they are essential in that they provide stability and endurance for society. In fact, because of their stability, institutions are able to give birth to new movements. The Church's strength as an institution has blessed its history with new movements spontaneously springing up.

In my brief life time, several movements have come and stayed, and some have come and gone or waned: among them the Christian Family Movement, Young Christian Students, Young Christian Workers, Cursillo, the Charismatic movement, the Catholic Worker movement, the Peace movement, the Pro-Life movement. New movements will develop in the future as in the past, and the mission of the Church will stay fresh, meeting new needs and responding to the Holy Spirit's impulse in fresh ways.

The Anchor of Compassion Will...

Keep you grounded in the Biblical call to act on the seven corporal works of mercy: feed the hungry, give drink to the thirsty, clothe the naked, visit the imprisoned, shelter the homeless, visit the sick, and bury the dead.

Connect you with the compassion of Jesus and bless you with the gifts that only the poor can give.

Bring joy to your heart as you are in appreciation of the Church's service to the poorest of the poor, in your parish, your diocese, your nation, and around the world.

Provide you with role models of real people who, with deep faith, sought to address human needs.

Catholic Practice - setting this anchor more firmly...

Choose an agency or some cause that you can support with prayers and financial help, no matter how small.

Subscribe to *Maryknoll* magazine, the *National Catholic Reporter*, *Our Sunday Visitor*, your diocesan newspaper, and other publications, to keep in touch with ministries meeting some of those needs.

Read the life and writings of Mother Teresa and check out the works of her religious order, the Missionaries of Charity.

Search Community of Sant' Egidio, Catholic Charities USA, Caritas International, Benedictine Order, DeLaSalle Christian Brothers, Brothers of Charles Lwanga, and others to learn about the rich history of Catholic response to people in need.

ON BENDED KNEE... My heart moves me to be grateful to Jesus for His words that have inspired so many followers to serve those in need. Thank You, Jesus, for showing us the heart of God, a heart filled with compassion and empathy, a heart eager to clothe the naked, visit the lonely, and feed the hungry. Give me eyes to see what you see in the anxiety of my brothers and sisters. Give me ears to hear the cries of those who suffer. Give me hands to help in the healing of broken and barren lives. When it should be my turn to receive, give me the graces of acceptance and gratitude. Amen.

ANCHOR TWO
Social Justice

Compassion (charity) is half of the equation. The other half is justice. A major contribution to humanity in recent centuries has been our doctrine on social justice. The individual's good and the common good are essentially conjoined which is why we get involved in the burning issues of the day. Social Justice is that combination of moral values and actions that create and sustain right relationships between individuals and groups.

Prophets of Justice

One of the minor prophets --they were called minor only because their books were small-- was **Amos**. He is recognized as the prophet of social justice because he was outspoken to the rich whom he saw grinding the heads of the poor into the dust. Due to their exploitation of the working poor, the wealthy were living luxuriantly while the poor went hungry, lacked shelter, and had nothing to live on. Amos shouted for justice and demanded that the poor be treated with dignity and fairness.

Amos became my hero in 1964 when I traveled with three other priests to the state of Mississippi. The Civil Rights movement was heating up then. I had helped organize a campaign which raised $20,000 in the Twin Cities to support voter registration efforts in the South. As the four of us drove into Mississippi with Minnesota license plates we were followed for two hours by a pick-up truck with two rifles purposely visible in its back window. The fact that civil rights workers from the North were being harassed, kidnapped, and murdered made that ride a tense one.

The prophet Amos had been criticized by the "red necks", the bigots of his time, for preaching against injustice across the border from his own country. "Go back to your own land," they shouted. "We don't have any trouble here." There seemed to be a clear parallel between Amos' time and ours. But as Amos did, so did the civil rights workers from the North. They stuck with their convictions and continued to work for justice even if far from home.

Then in 1965, I participated in the March led by **Dr. Martin Luther King Jr.** from Selma to Montgomery, Alabama. In many ways the Selma March was a turning point in the movement. King's commitment to peaceful protests made the experience especially intense as we (estimates as high as 50,000 marchers) were well aware of the dangers for "do-gooders' from the North. Amos was present in my thoughts throughout the four day experience. As the March entered Montgomery, the state capitol, where King would speak, armed soldiers faced outward along the way to protect us. I will never forget the angry faces and hate-filled shouts that were hurled from front porches of homes lining the streets. Wasn't Jesus a pacifist? Dorothy Day? Bishop Oscar Romero? Francis of Assisi? Is not every Christian called to trust in the power of love over hate, of peaceful protest over violence?

Being baptized into the Body of Christ, Christians are called to be prophetic, to speak out against injustice and work to establish justice. Our Church must be prophetic. It was very clearly so during the Industrial revolution. That era called for clarity in matters of justice between employer and employee. The foundation for Catholic Social Teaching was laid by Pope Leo XIII in 1891 with his classic encyclical letter titled Rerum Novarum, On the Condition of Workers. In it he set down basic principles of justice and social order that have periodically been updated by his successors.

Catholic Social Teaching

A personal story. I happened to be born during the Great Depression and was in grade school while the Second World War was going on. My dad had only two years of elementary school and my mother never went to high school. This was not all that untypical in those years, but my parents wanted their children to have a chance at success: hopefully get a decent job, buy a house, raise a family, and stay out of jail. To accomplish any of that they believed that their children, at least, had to get a high school diploma. They chose Cretin High School for me and my four brothers largely because of the excellent reputation of the Christian Brothers who staffed Cretin at the time.

My father worked at a coal foundry where Energy Park is now in St. Paul. The working conditions there were horrible, with thick smoke, air polluted heavily with gases, long working hours --during the World War II my dad had to work 16 hour days—low wages and few benefits. Being concerned about his family's future, he joined a labor union, and eventually received health insurance, a pension, workman's compensation, and some paid vacation time. But not without a struggle. Worker's strikes in those days often turned violent and people got hurt. Wealthy owners were not about to give in easily. Imagine the courage it took to walk picket lines and fight for justice.

My first exposure to a worker's strike was in 1948. I was twelve. My dad drove our family over to South St. Paul where some 10,000 workers were on strike, closing the meat packing plants for 67 days. This strike had gotten violent at times. I have never forgotten the sight of the National Guard, their tanks and armored vehicles, their guns at the ready, keeping things calm, as we sat in the car and watched from a nearby hill.

In Europe and the United States, the Catholic Church stood on the side of the working class since that was where the Gospel of justice had to be. Eventually, Industrialization brought a better life to millions of people, but early on a huge gap developed between Labor (the working class) and Capital (the Owners). The rich were getting richer and the poor poorer. The plight of the working class had hit bottom decades earlier when child labor had been the norm in the coal mines and factories of England. It was there that child labor first became illegal and education became mandatory for children. But there remained plenty of adults to be exploited. Life was very hard for the vast majority of people, which made the rise of the labor unions necessary.

Karl Marx and Russia offered a different answer to the worker's plight, atheistic communism. The battle between Catholic Social Teaching and atheistic Communism eventually resulted in communism's demise.

POPE LEO XIII'S encyclical letter had profound and lasting influence on history. Catholic Social Teaching strongly favored the right of workers to organize. A quick review of *Rerum Novarum* reveals a balanced and wise set of principles that have guided social justice advocates for more than a century. Listed next are some of these principles. To us today, many of them may seem obvious. They were not so at the end of the nineteenth century. As you read them, try to imagine the conditions that existed to make their explicit citation necessary.

- People are naturally entitled to the fruits of their labors.
- People have the right to acquire and own property and to dispose of it.
- Government exists for the public well-being of the people.
- Labor (work) is honorable. God gave the earth to humans for their needs.
- Humans must share wealth with others "when others are in need."
- Human greatness comes not from what people have but what they are.
- Wages must be just, adequate to secure a decent livelihood.
- It is immoral to make profits out of another's need.
- Workers and owners need each other and have duties toward each other.
- In extreme necessity the family has the right to call on the State for aid.
- When all else has failed, workers have a right to strike.
- The law should prevent conditions which bring on a strike.
- The law should favor private ownership.
- The right to strike is not the right to destroy.
- Taxation is not to be excessive.
- Child labor must be in accord with their strength and condition.
- The hours of labor must be short enough to allow for rest and recreation.
- Worker's spiritual interests must be safeguarded.

American students would do well to study the history of the Industrialization period before traveling to any Third World country. Where many Third World nations are today is where we were 100 and 150 years ago: wages insufficient to raise a family, dangerous working environments, no safety nets in case of injury or illness, no benefits such as paid vacations and pensions. The institution that should be preventing unjust exploitation of the poor is government, but in many poor nations it is often the corruption of governmental leaders that is feeding injustice. Among the forces that brought our recent generation a living wage, health benefits, pensions, workman's comp, paid vacations, and reasonable working hours has been our Church.

As I reflect on major contributions that Catholics have made in the development of American society, at least four major blessings come to mind. First, our Church has presented to the world a cohesive set of principles which brought Labor and Capital together to achieve justice for the working class (my father among them) while simultaneously respecting the roles that owners and government play in building up the common good. Second, the Church's respect for the human mind has resulted in the education of millions of citizens and immigrants, at its own expense, through its educational institutions from kindergarten to graduate school. Third, Catholic parishes have played a major role in stabilizing communities, encouraging high ideals and the best of moral and social behaviors in neighborhoods. Fourth, Catholic hospitals and other health facilities have brought medicine with heart throughout the land.

The Catholic commitment to social justice is really not a choice, if we are to take our Faith seriously. It is of the very constitution of the Church to work for justice. A term that has been promoted by the United States Bishops to designate this moral obligation is "preferential option for the poor." This is not new for Christians. Since New Testament times, followers of Jesus have answered the call to help individuals and groups in need. In recent centuries, dismantling unjust systems has become the goal of justice advocates as well. In every age Christian men and women have found service to the marginalized and impoverished to be their calling.

Seekers of Justice

In our own times, several Catholic seekers of justice have answered the call and made the ultimate sacrifice of their lives standing up for justice and the rights of the poor. Four nuns, a laywoman and two archbishops join the list of martyrs who committed themselves to social justice. More than how they died, they are noted for how they lived.

SR. DOROTHY STANG

SR. DOROTHY STANG, a member of the Sisters of Notre Dame de Namur, devoted her life to improving the lives of the poor in the Amazon region of Brazil. The Brazilian government had opened up thousands of acres for the poor to homestead on a small plot of land. Huge plots had been given to the wealthy for cattle raising and logging. Sr. Dorothy, along with two Italian priest missionaries and another nun followed the poor, forming small faith communities, teaching them their legal rights, and helping them to set up schools for their children and to organize unions for themselves. As in other areas of Latin America, justice and peace activists who were dedicated to assisting the poor, were labeled "communists" and harassed or worse, killed.

On Feb. 12, 2005, Sister Dorothy was halted by two gunmen who had been paid $25,000 by two ranchers to kill her. When they asked her if she had a weapon, she showed them her Bible and quoted three of the Beatitudes, including "Blessed are the peacemakers for they shall be called children of God." They gunned her down.

SISTERS ITA FORD, MAURA CLARKE, DOROTHY KAZAL AND JEAN DONOVAN

SISTERS ITA FORD, MAURA CLARKE, and **DOROTHY KAZAL**, along with church worker **JEAN DONOVAN**, were abducted, raped, and murdered in El Salvador on Dec. 2, 1980. They had dedicated their lives to help the poorest of the poor gain dignity and a decent livelihood. El Salvador at the time was in the midst of a civil war that eventually took an estimated 100,000 lives. In June, 1980, the women began working with the poor and with victims of the war, providing food, shelter, transportation and burial. Donovan had been a pallbearer for Archbishop Oscar Romero three months earlier, following his assassination because of his commitment to social justice. On Dec. 2 of that year, the four women were stopped by members of the National Guard, taken to an isolated location, tortured, raped, and murdered. These four women represent hundreds of Roman Catholic missionaries and local Church workers who are dedicated to the Gospel of Jesus Christ and the works of compassion and justice.

DOM HELDER CAMARA

Although **DOM HELDER CAMARA** (+ 1999) has not been declared a saint by the Church, he was embraced as such during his lifetime by the people he served. Permit me to introduce one of my heroes. In 1975, I introduced him to a huge crowd of Catholic teachers assembled in Minneapolis. At the time, Dom Helder was being harassed by the Brazilian government because of his outspoken support of the millions of poor he served. Recife, Brazil was one of the poorest cities in the world and Dom Helder, Archbishop of Recife, seemed to be the only hope for the impoverished masses. But he was controversial. He spoke out against the establishment, pushing for reform, even reform in the Church which had snuggled too closely with government leaders and the rich. He is quoted as saying, " When I gave food to the poor they called me a saint. When I asked *why* the poor were hungry, they called me a communist."

Dom Helder moved out of the Bishop's palatial residence into a simple room. His voice for justice and peace so outraged the leadership, they tried to silence him by assassinating some of his priests and closest co-workers. When he was nominated for the Nobel Peace prize and passed over, a separate prize of nearly one quarter of a million dollars was raised through the aegis of the World Council of Churches, a Protestant organization. He used the money to build housing in the poorest slums of Recife.

Archbishop Camara had issues with the institutional Church. He wanted the hierarchy (Pope and Bishops) to abandon their medieval garb and dress more simply. He encouraged them to win back the virtue of pover- ty. His poetry and speeches reveal a deeply spiritual man, rooted in the Gospel of non-violence, and a witness to the compassion of Jesus and absolute necessity of justice.

ARCHBISHOP OSCAR ROMERO

Another apostle to the poor in Latin America was **ARCHBISHOP OSCAR ROMERO**. The movie, *Romero*, is a powerful exposition of the chal- lenge a bishop has when both the poor and the rich, the powerful and the disenfranchised, are members of his flock. Romero's personal journey is an unforgettable demonstration of God's grace active in the midst of violence and injustice on the road to peace. Assassinated in 1980 while offering Mass, Romero lives on in the memories of Salvadorans and beyond as they, like him, commit themselves to make justice happen for people stuck in poverty.

THE BISHOPS OF THE UNITED STATES speak regularly to issues of justice in their role as proclaimers of the Gospel of Jesus Christ. Their documents, available on line or through the United States Catholic Conference, provide thoughtful reflections and directives on such issues as race relations, poverty, the urban crisis, abortion, economic justice, home ownership, political responsibility, education, the elderly, handicapped, agriculture, capital punishment and health care.

> A story is told about a man who saw dead bodies floating down the river. He began to pull them out and give them decent burials. Days later, exhausted from the endless flow of bodies, he decided to go up river, find out the cause of these deaths, and fix the problem. This story came to mind one day when I was reading a diatribe against Mother Teresa's care of the people dying in the streets of Calcutta. "Why doesn't she address the cause and fix the problem, then she wouldn't have to deal with people dying in the streets?" The complaint struck me as wrong-headed. In real life, there will be a need for someone down river to care for the wounded, sick, and dying, and someone upstream tackling the injustice that caused the hurt in the first place. Both compassion and justice must be on the Church's agenda.

The previous chapter focused on compassion and offered a glimpse of countless ministries that serve the sick, wounded, and dying, the work of mercy and compassion down river. This chapter's focus has been the work that is essentially upriver, the pursuit of systemic justice. Some Catholic agencies specialize in alleviating suffering while others seek to prevent it in the first place. For Catholics in Minnesota, the agency that specializes in systemic justice is the Minnesota Catholic Conference. Many dioceses have similar organizations. These conferences speak to a variety of issues in education, immigration, marriage and family, emergency assistance for people living on the edge of society, children and community services, residential group homes, and assistance with rent. Basically they address any issue that affects the common good and the dignity of person.

In sum, Catholic social teaching as practiced by the Church is vitally interested and involved in seven areas: Dignity of work and rights of workers, option for the poor and vulnerable, universal solidarity, care for God's creation, life and dignity of the human person, responsibility for family and community, and rights and responsibilities of the human person.

THE ANCHOR OF SOCIAL JUSTICE WILL...

Inspire you to pursue the common good.

Arouse a just anger in you when you see flagrant violations of justice, and energize you to get involved and work for justice.

Prevent you from taking advantage and exploiting others if ever the temptation should arise.

Give you the Gospel's perspective on politics and religion.

Inform your vote whenever justice issues are addressed.

Inspire you to study more fully the dynamics of systemic change, both in history and current times.

CATHOLIC PRACTICE – SETTING THIS ANCHOR MORE FIRMLY...

Look up some of the Catholic "giants" for social justice, e.g. Dorothy Day, Msgr. John A. Ryan, Msgr. George Higgins, Dom Helder Camara, Sr. Rita Steinhagen, Oscar Romero, Vincent de Paul, Mother Cabrini, Sr. Helen Prejean, Sr. Thea Bowman.

Read the letter of John Paul II on Women (Try to read it from the perspective of women in Third World countries where women's rights are woefully neglected.) Also, *Mulieris Dignitatem: Dignity and Vocation of Women* by John Paul II.

Acquaint yourself with Leo XIII's encyclical, Rerum Novarum and its basic principles of justice, peace and the social order.

Review the teaching about Just War found in the Catholic Catechism

Memorize the Peace Prayer of St. Francis.

Study the Economic and Peace pastoral letters of the Catholic Bishops of the United States.

Read: The life of Sr. Dorothy Stang, SNDdeN, by Sr. Roseanne Murphy, SNDdeM

ON BENDED KNEE... Prayer of St. Francis
Lord, make me an instrument of your peace. Where there is hatred let me sow love; where there is injury, pardon; where there is doubt, faith; where there is despair, hope; where there is darkness, light; and where there is sadness, joy. O Divine Master, grant that I may not so much seek to be consoled, as to console; to be understood as to understand, to be loved as to love. For it is in giving that we receive; It is in pardoning that we are pardoned; It is dying that we are born to eternal life. Amen.

ANCHOR THREE
Moral Tradition

We have a moral tradition that has withstood the test of time.
Believing in the ten commandments and in Jesus'
commandment of love, we stand on a firm moral foundation.
Made in God's image we are called to love God
and to do good as passionately as Jesus did.

The Decalogue

The Ten Commandments are timeless in their application. In the Western part of the world they are the basis of our society and of the laws of our lands. Here they are as taught in our Catholic tradition. Each commandment, even when stated negatively promotes a positive value.

The First: I am The Lord Thy God
Thou Shall Not Have False Gods Before Me

At its core, this commandment tells a most fundamental truth. There is only one God who created all things, including humans, and this one God deserves our gratitude and respect. We humans are strange but wonderful creatures. We can think ourselves into believing that we are sufficient unto ourselves and do not need to bow to anyone else. We have the capacity to place our trust in "other gods" like fun, fame, and fortune. Doing so means that we would prefer to establish the foundation of our lives on a lie. Not too smart! So, this commandment tells us to put God first and other things will fall into their proper place.

The Second: Thou Shalt Not
Take The Name of The Lord In Vain

Making an oath while using God as our witness is not how God wants to be used. Think of it. Would you like to be trivialized? Using God's name with anything less than complete reverence is disrespectful of the One to whom we not only owe our lives but everything in our lives. Would you use your father's or mother's names with anything less than reverence? It is not that God needs our respect. We need to respect God. It is for our good, not God's, that this commandment and all the others exist. This commandment calls us to have reverence for God in the way that the Maker of all things ought to be treated. Words have power. Cursing, swearing, speaking without respect for our Creator in a real sense pollutes the atmosphere. Not only does it negatively influence those within earshot, but it also returns to the speaker and taints his or her love for God.

THE THIRD: KEEP HOLY THE LORD'S DAY

For more than three thousand years members of the Jewish faith, and for two thousand years members of the Christian faith have kept one day a week as holy. For our Jewish brothers and sisters, Saturday is their holy day, beginning the eve before. Jesus observed the Saturday Sabbath as the holy day of his faith. But then, because He rose from the dead on the "first day of the week", a Sunday, His followers shifted their Sabbath observance from Saturday to Sunday. For us Catholics, Sunday is our holy day, beginning the evening before. That is why attendance at Sunday liturgy is a serious obligation for us. Again, this commandment is not for God's good, but for ours. We need one day a week for worship and rest if we are to keep our priorities straight, especially in the busy world we live in today.

THE FOURTH: HONOR YOUR FATHER AND MOTHER

If the first three commandments are given to us to safeguard our relationship with God, the ensuing seven are given to us to safeguard our relationships with ourselves and other people. The most basic relationship we humans have is with our parents. While we are young and responsible to our parents, we are called to obedience. It's as simple as that. We may think we have better ideas than our parents, and they may well be better, but better is not the deal breaker here. When we feel resistance building up, that's the time to bite the bullet and obey.

Though it can be difficult for teens to admit, parents do have greater wisdom and experience. The only time we are morally obliged to disobey our parents is when they order us to do something evil, like stealing or harming another. The fourth commandment also applies when our parents get older, when the obligation of parenting shifts and we become their caretakers. A further extension of this commandment is its application to the human family as it calls for respect toward all legitimate authority, religious and civil.

THE FIFTH: THOU SHALT NOT KILL

Either thyself or another person, either all at once or gradually! Think about it. Each commandment is given to us for our own good. Each one protects something valuable and necessary for the social welfare of individuals and communities. For years the cigarette industry claimed that smoking was not harmful to health and so it became one of the most common methods of killing people gradually. Drugs, alcohol, and addictions (e.g. to work and food) also can kill over time. This commandment orders us to treat ourselves and others rightly, respecting the gifts of health and well-being that God wants for us. Obviously, murder, euthanasia, abortion, and genocide are examples of actions that kill "all at once," that is, quickly. In a word, the fifth commandment protects human life and seeks its well being in all situations and stages of life.

Deliberately toying with danger -- for example, speeding, texting while driving, experimenting with drugs – also violates this commandment. You may ask: what about war and police protection? Is some killing justified? Good questions which the Church has wrestled with for centuries and arrived at some answers. Check these out in the Catholic Catechism. Also, check out why Catholic morality is against the death penalty.

THE SIXTH: THOU SHALT NOT COMMIT ADULTERY

Adultery is one of the most hurtful of human actions. The trust between husband and wife that the marriage commitment calls for is shattered by infidelity. The relationship between husband and wife is the most basic and time honored relationship in the history of humankind. The God-given good that this commandment protects are human relationships, especially family, friendship, parent-child, and dating.

There is a wonderful saying: the greatest gift a father can give his children is to love their mother. And vice versa for the mother's gift to her children. This commandment calls us to respect our sexuality for the creative and intimate purposes God has placed in it. All world religions place great value on marital fidelity and the self-discipline fidelity requires both in and outside of marriage. Since the "sexual revolution" of the Sixties, Christian sexual moral norms have been challenged by attitudes promoting casual and recreational sex. The Christian ethic states that sexual activity is moral only within the commitment of marriage.

THE SEVENTH: THOU SHALT NOT STEAL

Nothing destroys trust more in neighborhoods, workplaces, homes, schools, athletic teams, drama groups, or between friends than stealing, cheating, being dishonest. Trust is the value that this commandment protects. Today's grandparent generation grew up at a time when people could leave the doors of their homes and garages unlocked, even at night. They did not have to worry about robbers and intruders. They did not have to lock their cars or padlock their bikes. The virtue of trust was not only valued, but observed throughout the community. When trust is weak, fears grow, more laws have to be passed, more cops have to patrol the streets, and the feeling of safety that everyone has a right to, weakens. This commandment is global in outreach, calling for justice in local and global economies and fair play between individuals and groups.

THE EIGHTH: THOU SHALT NOT BEAR FALSE WITNESS

This commandment also values trust. Honesty is the only way to go in human relationships, especially when the truth is critical to the health and well being of another. Imagine the damage done by harmful gossip or when outright lies are told about an innocent person. Imagine the damage done when the lies are on the witness stand of a courtroom and an innocent person goes to prison unjustly. This commandment calls us to grow strong in moral character so that we can live our lives with integrity. One lie leads to another. In the same way, one honest act leads to another.

Honesty is the best policy, as the saying goes, and, yes, there can be situations when prudence requires the withholding of truth, for example, when the one seeking a response has no right to it. Honesty isn't always as simple as it sounds. But it is the best foundation for life and for healthy relationships. As with all virtues, honesty is built into one's moral character by being honest, time after time. It's like a brick wall, built into something solid, one brick after another.

THE NINTH: THOU SHALT NOT COVET ANOTHER'S WIFE

To covet is to want something so badly that you would do anything to get it. The great biblical character, King David, coveted the wife of one of his soldiers so badly he not only had Bathsheba's husband killed but, also, in the deed done, lost his integrity and peace of conscience for the rest of his life. Coveting is more than just an inkling of a thought, more than "Gee, I sure would like to meet this gorgeous woman or handsome man." To covet is to want so badly that one is willing to sin boldly to have it. Not good for the people involved, not good for families and neighborhoods, and not good for society at large.

THE TENTH: THOU SHALT NOT COVET THY NEIGHBOR'S GOODS

Same thing here. So, your friend has an i-pod that you would like to have. You covet it so intensely that you find a way to steal it, or you simply couldn't help yourself when you stole one at the mall. Sorry. The excuse will not stand up in court (nor in God's court!) This commandment says: watch your "wants". Stay in control. If you don't, you may end up behaving badly and that won't be good for you, your victim, or the community at large. Society needs good people so people need to be good. Remember: a chain is as strong as its weakest link!

From Ten Commandments to Two: Ultimately to One Word

The Decalogue or Ten Commandments have been criticized by some as negative. Some Christians wrongly prefer to believe that the Old Testament God is a mean cantankerous judge while the God of the New Testament is loving and kind, and that Old Testament morality is a bunch of negatives. If you think this, take another look. Each one of the ten commandments protects a positive value: reverence for our Creator God, respect for God's name and things holy, worship of God as the foundational principle for an ordered life, the parent-child relationship, health and well-being, sexuality, trust, respect for property and people.

When Jesus was asked which commandment was the greatest He taught that there is really only one commandment. Love God with your whole heart and mind, and love your neighbor as yourself which really is a summary of the classical Ten. Still another summary is simply the word **Love**. That is what it all gets down to. Love.

So, what is sin? The classical meaning of the word is "missing the mark." God made us and knows the targets of moral behavior that lead to our happiness and the common good of the human race. Having blessed us with freedom (otherwise we could not truly love God in return, or anyone else for that matter) we can choose to aim at the target or not. Sin is the choice to miss a target, honesty, for example, or chastity, or reverence, or obedience, and the other virtues.

The word "inappropriate", when used to describe a moral wrong, is not the correct descriptive. Sin is a faith word, steeped in the Jewish and Christian traditions. As a faith word it acknowledges God as the One whose moral target we have missed while committing an immoral act. "Inappropriate" may be the appropriate word to describe my failure to remove my cap during the national anthem, for example, since that act violates a social norm not a moral one, but it is not adequate to describe my stealing from another. Theft is a moral wrong which, when I think about it as a believer in God, is also correctly labeled a sin. The word sin acknowledges God's rightful place in our moral choices.

Making good choices:
The challenge for teens and young adults

The term "at risk" has usually referred to teens dealing with drugs, alcohol abuse, gangs, and similar life situations. But in reality, all teens are "at risk". Consider this. Now able to take pictures of the developing brain, modern medicine has determined that, contrary to earlier understandings that the human brain was fully developed by age seventeen, the human brain continues to grow into the mid twenties. And it's the pre-frontal cortex that is still growing during late adolescence and young adulthood.

So what does this part of the brain do? Executive function. That is, it's that part of the brain that makes decisions and judgments, that differentiates among conflicting thoughts, that determines good and bad, better and best. It presents future consequences of present actions, and helps us work toward goals that are defined. It also predicts outcomes from current behaviors, and applies social control (suppressing urges that if not suppressed, could lead to socially unacceptable outcomes.) In adolescents, the pre-frontal cortex is not there yet. Which is why adolescents need parents, mentors, and friends to help them make good decisions about speed limits, texting while driving, binge drinking, pornography, premarital sexual behaviors, sexually transmitted diseases and the limitations of safer sex, drug use, hanging around with the wrong crowd, and jumping off cliffs. A challenge for all parents and parental surrogates (teachers, coaches, employers, etc.) is to save us from ourselves as we go through adolescence.

Here are some situations that are off shoots to the "pre-frontal cortex" reality.

- "But we love each other" ends up with him or her being used and both more confused about what love truly is.

- Sex, drugs, alcohol, erratic thinking and doing, have a way of derailing us on our way to maturity. Hi-jacking, subtle and not-so-subtle, is another apt description of the effects of poor decision making. In a hi-jacking, an enemy takes you to places you really do not want to go!

- Sexually active teenage girls are four times more likely to experience depression than girls who are not sexually active. For boys, the ratio is two times more likely.

- Having life goals, that is, a career and life purpose to aim at, helps significantly in our making good decisions during adolescence. The fact is that not only are high school students undecided about long term choices, but also vast numbers of college students do not have firm decisions about their future.

- "How can something that feels so good possibly be bad" is a question most teens are not yet ready to be wise about. The power of passion, the "love is blind" phenomenon, the lure of "feeling high" get in the way of seeing reality as it is.

- The brain damage caused by chemical abuse is not the first thing on an adolescent's mind when he or she is floating in mid-air. That's long term damage. The immediate damage may instead be accidents, date rape, acts of vandalism and even death.

- "If I get in trouble, medications will fix me." When we are young we tend to harbor the feeling of invulnerability, thinking that every hurt can be healed and that we can survive any risk we take. Knowledge about long-term side-effects may not be enough to prevent destructive behaviors. The distance between the head and the heart (knowing what's right and choosing it) can be especially difficult for adolescents to bridge.

Since sexual development is critically significant during adolescence, other factors that have an impact on wholesome development are important to consider. One of these factors is the preponderance of **peer pressure**, putting all teens and young adults "at risk". Our identities (sexual and core identities) typically do not settle for life until the mid twenties. That is when, hopefully for all, we have reached a personal authenticity, with our morals and values pretty well established for life, and a strong sense of self, making us capable of making good choices in a mature manner. The leap from friend to lover is huge and sets teens up for unwise choices. "Everybody is doing it" may be the popular mantra, but a false one. Current data indicate that today's teens are less likely to be sexually active than a decade ago. Fact or not, majority rule is not a valid basis for morality.

Another factor making all adolescents "at risk" is the **over-stimulation** in our culture. So much of the media that dominates adolescents' lives is driven by greed, created and promoted by immature adults and shabby role models, fueled by readily available pornography and other negative, shallow, and false values. Add to this, anti-religious sentiments which serve to sever adolescents' ties to highly principled communities.

Still another factor is that adolescents are on the way but **not there yet** in their capacity to understand the relationship between love and sex, the responsibilities that come with adult behaviors, the interplay of gender similarities and gender differences (e.g. that males may tend to play at love in order to have sex, and females may tend to play at sex looking for love.)

Many teens, perhaps most, seem to understand their "at risk" phase of growth and appreciate and work with the adults in their lives. These young folks will survive the risks with a few minor scars. Others, more resistant to external controls, benefit greatly from adults who hang in there with them, seeing them through their hurting and healing, continuing to provide encouragement and guidance, offering honest feedback, and persist in loving them while not approving certain behaviors. Adults know from their own experiences that new beginnings are usually possible, that some past mistakes may leave permanent scars but scars can serve as a warning in future situations.

There is no substitute for genuine moral strength. A moral fabric that is founded upon faith in Jesus Christ will serve us well throughout life, until shadows fall and our journey ends. The one thing no one can take from us is integrity. We need to cherish it.

FRIENDSHIP HAS ITS RULES

During adolescence, the major task in personal development is the I-Thou, person to person, the one-to-one relationship, growing in our capacity to form healthy relationships. For adolescents, friendship is the field of play most critical to this development.

To have friends, you have to be a friend. In other words you have to be caring, thoughtful, faithful, honest, trusting, available, and hospitable to your friends and you have the right to expect the same from them.

Friends don't let friends drive while drunk! In other words, friends take appropriate responsibility for the safety and welfare of their friends. They do what they should to protect and defend them. True friends say what their friends need to hear not what they might want to hear.

Friends respect appropriate boundaries of privacy, keeping confidences, avoiding gossip.

Friends strive to bring out the best in each other. They want the best for their friend.

Friends let their friends have other friends! Friendship is not ownership, not a possessive and exclusive relationship. Cherish friends but do not smother them!

Once friends have sex they can never go back to just being friends. Sex changes the relationship forever. The leap from friend to lover is real and a big one.

"Friends with benefits", that is, a relationship of consensual casual sex with little or no commitment, impedes healthy sexual development and is morally wrong. A sad result of this approach to sex is the added difficulty later in life to establish a genuine and intimate relationship when sex needs to be in the service of love.

The Anchor of Moral Tradition Will...

Bring you the inner peace that comes from doing the right thing because it is the right thing to do.

Give you the satisfaction that comes with relationships built on mutual reverence, trust, and a chaste love.

Serve as the foundation for justice and fairness in your relationships and responsibilities.

Give you the peace of mind knowing that the wisdom of the ages, born of struggle and triumph, guides your behaviors.

Give you the strength you will need to avoid the temptations that denigrate your integrity such as pornography, dishonesty, infidelity, fornication, abuse of alcohol and drugs.

Catholic Practice – setting this anchor more firmly...

Memorize the Ten Commandments, and the one commandment of Jesus.

Resolve to become and to be a person of strong moral integrity. Commit to living the positive values underlying the Ten Commandments, and the Gospel values of Jesus.

Choose reverence as your way of life; reverence for yourself (body and spirit), reverence toward all of God's creation and things holy.

Choose to be above any fashion, behavior or trend that fails to respect you as a child of God and a follower of Jesus. Take a stand against violence, sexualization of both males and females, and the crass materialism that can infiltrate our lives.

Read about and reflect on how to be a friend. Find friends who share your values.

Make a practice of regular reception of the Sacrament of Reconciliation. Advent and Lent are appropriate times to make a confession and receive absolution. In Confession, it is Jesus who forgives through the ministry of the Church, made visible in sight and sound with a priest confessor.

On bended knee...Lord Jesus, I come before You this day, aware that You call me to live the high ideals of Your Gospel. Let me not be faint, nor indifferent, toward your invitation. If I am strong in virtue, the world around me will be blessed. If I am firm in my convictions, others will be strengthened to do good as well. Take me as I am but expand your life within me. Amen.

ANCHOR FOUR
Jesus
In History, Mystery and Majesty

Jesus is the center of Christianity.
We are Christians, disciples of Jesus Christ, believers in the
One whom God has sent to show us how great is the
Almighty's love for us. Re-born into His Spirit we are called to
community and to live out our lives as members of
His Mystical Body on earth.

So, who is Jesus anyway?

No need to try to prove or disprove that He actually lived on this earth. It's well documented and not seriously challenged. So, he lived, a person of historical significance, mentioned even in some secular documents. And he died, a criminal's death. And His followers claimed He was raised from the dead and is now "seated at the right hand of God in heaven."

The question of faith before you is this: will you believe in Jesus Christ as your Lord and Savior? Will you accept Him as the One whom God has sent to bring healing and hope to the world?

To grasp the significance of this faith question, let's look at Jesus from three perspectives: history, mystery, and majesty. Recall the acclamation: *Christ has died (history), Christ is Risen (mystery), Christ will come again (majesty.)*

History

If you ever wondered why God did not take on a human form until the middle of the Roman era, think of a line in Paul's letter to the Galatians (4:4): "In the fullness of time, when God sent his Son, born of a woman, …" In the fullness of time! Prior to this era humanity had not developed to the point where historical records could be fashioned and the known world could receive the "Good news" about such a God-event as the birth of Jesus. When conditions were right, God chose Mary of Nazareth to be the bearer of a child who would be named Jesus and who would bring salvation to humankind.

Salvation? What is meant by that? Simply put, salvation is the gift offered to every human person which is to believe in God, have a personal relationship with Jesus, and be given the gift of "eternal life", that is, the experience of seeing God, face to Face, soul to Soul, for ever. This gift is beyond the possibility of description. "Eye has not seen nor ear heard what God has in store for those who love Him." (I Cor. 2:9)

But salvation comes in here-and-now forms as well. The teachings of Jesus show exceptional wisdom and answer many of the questions and dilemmas in life. They inspire us in the midst of suffering, they get us moving in the right direction when complexity or barriers rear their troublesome heads. His words bring light to dispel darkness, they bring healing to hurt, hope to despair, forgiveness to resentment, love to hate, moderation to indulgence, faith to doubt, and much, much more.

Pick up the Gospel of St. Matthew and ponder chapters 5, 6 and 7, the Sermon on the Mount. The Beatitudes are loaded with hope. Jesus calls us the light of the world, the salt of the earth. That's looking at life with positive vibes! Then He challenges us to embrace the highest of ideals: genuine reconciliation and harmony with others, unadulterated fidelity in marriage, profound reverence for God and things holy, love of enemies, selfless generosity, humility in prayer and fasting. There's more!

He asks us to refrain from judging others, to trust in God's love whenever we feel anxious. He encourages us to pray with confidence and ask for anything. We need to be aware of false prophets. He tells us that we can't serve two masters, so choose to serve God rather than worldly possessions. We must build our spiritual house on rock not on sand so that when the winds and rains come we shall stand firm. **Jesus is the human voice of God.**

But Jesus is also the human face of God. As we ponder His life, to whom He paid attention, His activity and life work, His compassion and forgiving heart, His spirit of hospitality and commitment to justice, and His unconditional love, we realize how much God loves us. In Jesus we see the face of God.

Time and again, in the presence of illness, the compassion of God guided His healing touch. In the presence of loneliness and exclusion, He welcomed the outcasts, assuring them of their worth in God's eyes. When He was betrayed by Peter and Judas, His friends and disciples, He offered forgiveness and a fresh start while respecting their free will. Jesus' time on earth was time enough to reveal clearly what God's original vision of humanity's purpose and final destination were, ultimate union with God.

Jesus is the human voice and the human face of our Creator God, whom He loved to call "Father." His teachings and the witness of His life continue to bless humanity in the *Mystery* of His Presence. You are living the *Mystery* now. Let's take a look at that word and its meaning in our Catholic experience.

Mystery

The word Mystery needs some explanation. Catholic tradition uses this term to designate the saving work of God in Jesus from the time of Pentecost to the end of the world. It is a far different meaning from its use in literature when it refers to stories with a mysterious plot or ending. Our use of the term here is far different.

Stated another way, **the Mystery is that great spiritual reality of God's saving work being accomplished, day after day, century after century, *with* Jesus, *through* Him and *in* Him during the centuries of "in-between" time.** This "in-between time" is the time in between the coming of the Holy Spirit at Pentecost and when Christ will return at the end of the world. We live in the Mystery of God's saving love with Jesus.

When Jesus celebrated the ritual meal of the Jews at the Last Supper, He gave his disciples a command. They were to take bread and wine, pray the blessings, and share a memorial ritual meal. After He said the blessings and shared the blessed bread and wine with those present, He told them: "Do this in memory of me." And so we do this in memory of Him. In our Roman Catholic tradition, celebration of the sacrament of the Eucharist is at the center of our faith. We believe that Jesus is present in sacred signs and sacraments. This cannot be stressed too much. In fact, our faith teaches us that it is Jesus who baptizes, Jesus who forgives sins, Jesus who is the

Priest accomplishing every sacrament. The ordained priest we know and see is acting in the name of Jesus and in the name of the Church, doing what Jesus asks of His followers.

There is only one priest, and that is Jesus, who, on the cross was both priest and victim. He is the one who has accomplished and continues to accomplish the union of humans with God. The primary role of priesthood is to join humanity with divinity. And Jesus continues to do this until the end of time, as He is present in and through the Church, the community of the baptized.

What many Catholics do not realize is that *Baptism confers priesthood.* So, every baptized person is one with the priesthood of Jesus. By our baptism we are one with Jesus in His offering of His sacrifice to the Father. There is but one sacrifice, Jesus, and one priest, Jesus. We are one priesthood with Christ Jesus. When we were baptized we were anointed as "priest, prophet and king", one with Christ in these roles. Catholic tradition refers to this as the Priesthood of the faithful. As Jesus selected certain of His followers to be Apostles, He gave them the responsibility to be servant leaders of the Church. As the Church grew, they called others to share in their service to the community of faith, thus the ordination of presbyters (priests) and deacons.

Word and Sacrament

The **mystery** that we were baptized into is sustained and nourished in two primary ways, Word and Sacrament. The word "Word" refers first to Jesus who is received as the Word of God, the revelation of the Almighty Creator God. The word "Word" also refers to the whole body of revealed writings, the Bible, which, though written by humans in human language, contains God's revelations to humanity. The most awesome revelation by God, however, is Jesus. He is *the Word* God has spoken, a Word that reveals in human flesh the love our Creator God has for us.

God's written revelation to humankind began with Genesis, the first book of the Bible, and continues in the whole of the Hebrew scriptures (which many Catholics will know as the Old Testament). God's revelation continued in the Christian Scriptures, or New Testament. These sacred writings we hold as revelations from God, God revealing truth to humankind in the exciting context of a faithful covenant. This God-human relationship began with Abraham and Sarah when God chose to walk with humans in the community of the first chosen people, the Jews. They continue their covenant while we, following Jesus, keep another covenant with God, the Christian covenant. It has taken a long time for us Catholics to appreciate our relationship to our Jewish brothers and sisters, but God has led us to this realization in our own time and beautiful results are coming from it.

Not all Christians interpret the Bible in the same way. Some insist on a literal interpretation. For these folks, for example, God created the universe in seven days exactly, that is, literally as it is written in the first book of Genesis. For others, Catholics among them, the creation story is neither science nor history. Yet it is as true as any revelation from God. The truths that this story reveals are first, that God created the universe. It did not happen by itself. Second, that God's creation is good. And third, that God entrusted the universe to humanity to use and to care for. In other words, the Bible is a faith book, it is God's hand writing but in human terms and experience. It is the account of God's walking with humanity, first with the Jewish community of faith, then with the community of faith founded by Jesus.

Both Scripture and Tradition

In Catholic understanding, God's revelation to humanity will continue to the end of time in two forms, Scripture and Tradition. The Bible is a holy Book and is to be revered as such. It is one of the two primary ways in which God speaks to humanity. The other is Tradition with a capital T. Tradition is the on-going presence of God's Spirit in the Church, a journey of obedience to God's revealing Presence. (The word, obedience, comes from the Latin *ob audire* which means to listen with the heart.) So, the Church and the Bible go hand in hand. The scriptures were born out of the community of faith, that is, the believing community of faith was there first, and the inspired writings grew out of its lived faith. And then the scriptures became the source which gave birth to new believers. The scriptures and the believing, living Church are essential to each other. In fact, the scriptures need the Church to guide, guard and unfold its meaning and revelation. And the Church needs Scripture to keep it on track.

What is so powerful about the Sacred Scriptures is that they have nourished the community of faith ever since they were written. Having been born out of the community of believers, they continue to give birth to new believers and inspiration to committed believers. A marvelous circle.

As important as the scriptures are in revealing God to us, however, God's most awesome revelation is Jesus. He is the Word whom God has spoken. In fact and in faith, the Gospel of John says it this way:

> *"In the beginning was the Word, and the Word was with God and the Word was God. He was in the beginning with God. All things came into being through Him, and without Him not one thing came into being.... And the Word became flesh and lived among us, and we have seen his glory, the glory as of a father's only son, full of grace and truth."*

We believe, accept and cherish Jesus as the Word of God, the Son of God, the One anointed by God to be our Savior and Redeemer, the One who has taken on our human nature so that we would not miss the principal revelation of God, namely, the Good News of God's love for us and for all of creation.

And so, **Jesus is the primary manifestation of God's revelation to humankind.** He is Sacrament Itself, a visible sign of God's saving love, the Word become human.

Permit me to share a personal experience when the presence of Jesus gave me a deep inner peace in the midst of great uncertainty and fear. I was a young priest totally given to the mission of ministering to adolescents. My style of work was Type A, describing in those days as the kind of person who had a dozen things going at once and was driven to accomplish. Then, on Ash Wednesday, 1978, my doctors informed me that I needed a coronary heart by-pass operation. The news was devastating. My first reaction was to get angry at God. After all, I was working my heart out (literally) for Jesus and the mission of the Church. Now this? Where is God? How can God do this to me?

My anger lasted about a month. During that time, some friends tried to console me, tried to help me see my way through this disappointment. I looked for light in the darkness that I had been plunged into. Some light came from the doctors as they shared data and experiences with the procedure that gave some hope. Some help came from friends, especially one who had survived the ordeal and was doing well.

But the most significant help came from a passage in Paul's letter to the Romans: "Whether we live or die, we are the Lord's". That line filled my mind with understanding and my heart with peace. It continues to this day to be a source of light in the darkness.

The evening before I entered the hospital to have heart surgery, I was in the audience at a concert raising funds for youth ministry. I had invited my mother and several other family members to join me. Of course I was nervous about the next day's surgery, and was feeling major uncertainty and a deep anxiety. Just before intermission the lead musician announced that their next song was being dedicated to "Fr. John Forliti who is having surgery tomorrow". Then they began to sing "On Eagle's Wings" a masterpiece composed by a former student of mine, Michael Joncas.

What happened next was a most unusual experience of God's loving presence. I felt lifted out of my seat, totally surrounded by a blanket of warmth. I did not even feel the seat I had been sitting in. I felt held by some spiritual Presence. Time seemed to stop. And I knew that whatever happened with the surgery, I would be okay, I would be in God's hands. If it failed and I died, I would be okay. If it was successful and I lived, I would be okay. It was another affirmation of Romans 14:8. "Whether we live or die we are the Lord's." Jesus was walking with me, present in the Mystery of God's saving love.

Yes, you and I live in the "in-between" time, the time between the first Pentecost when Jesus sent the Holy Spirit of God into the world and the time of the world's end. We are part of the Mystery of God's saving Presence, part of the countless numbers of believers, both past and future.

It is in this "in-between time" that God's Spirit is at work, inspiring, healing, instructing, forgiving, and caring. We Catholics do not see our life in the Spirit as our exclusive blessing, given only to us. For a long time, especially as a reaction to the Protestant reformers of the 16th century, we were blind to God's Presence in the "non-Catholics" of the world. But, eventually we were led to see God's activity in other communities of faith as well as our own. We have come to appreciate anew our calling to be a servant people with a unique part to play in God's walk with humanity.

We are called to live the Mystery of God's saving grace in such a way that all of humanity is blessed by our faithful response to the call of Jesus to build here on earth a reign of justice, peace, forgiveness and love. Like the twelve Apostles of long ago, some days we do pretty well, other days not so. Regardless, we are called.

Majesty

Christ has died, Christ is risen, Christ will come again. Our faith teaches us that there will be an end of the world, and that Jesus has been given the task of bringing God's plan for the world to fulfillment. This event has been given various names: an Armageddon, the rapture, the second and final coming of Jesus, the end of the world.

Several passages from the Christian scriptures describe the final coming, some of them in Jesus' own words. "They will see the Son of Man coming in a cloud with power and great glory." (Luke 21:27) "Then he will send out his angels, and gather his elect from the four winds, from the ends of the earth to the heavens." (Mark13:27). The most descriptive passage is when Jesus tells about the Son of Man, seated on his throne, having "the nations" gathered before him. He will separate them as a shepherd separates sheep from goats. To those on his right he will say, "Come, enter the kingdom my Father has prepared for you, because when I was hungry you gave me to eat, thirsty and you gave me to drink, naked and you clothed me." They will ask when they did those acts of kindness and Jesus will say "As long as you did it to a poor person you did it to me."

The term "majesty" in the threefold theme of history, mystery and majesty comes from the biblical scenes envisioning Jesus' return at the end of the world much like the climactic and dramatic return of a royal figure to his or her people. As I have attempted to grasp the fuller meaning of my faith, this threesome works for me. But so does another triple theme, namely, Christmas, Easter, and Pentecost.

At Christmas time we celebrate the birth of Jesus, that profound and sacred moment when God took on human form, the moment of history. At Easter time we celebrate the promise of life to be lived forever in God when Christ Jesus comes again to unite us with our Creator God forever, the moment of majesty. At Pentecost, we celebrate the Presence of God's Spirit living with us in these "in-between" times, our living in the mystery of God's saving Presence.

Many of the images of the final times are written in the book of Revelation, the last book of the Christian Bible. Written in highly poetic and mystical language, its descriptions of the end times are graphic. The writer has a vision of a new heaven and a new earth, "for the first heaven and earth had passed away." At that and forever after, God will dwell with his people, wiping every tear from their eyes. Death will be no more. God will make a new creation that will enjoy everlasting life.

Is this believable? If God can make the universe from nothing and set it in a development plan to the grandeur it is, why cannot God create a new creation which lasts from now and forever?

Go one step further. If God can create the universe as modern day science has discovered it, why could not God create other universes, populated by other living, thinking creatures? Aliens, for example? Why not?

We come back to the faith question. Do you believe in Jesus as your Lord and Savior, the One whom God has sent to show you the Way to the good life, and to Truth as best that you can know it? And do you believe in the Church as the Mystical Body of Jesus, called to be a living sign of God's saving Presence in the midst of the world?

WHY CHOOSE JESUS AS AN ANCHOR IN YOUR LIFE?

You do not have to look elsewhere to find the way to intimacy with the God who made you. Jesus is the One whom God has sent. He is the Savior of the world.

His teachings provide inspiration, direction, guidance, and wisdom...Anchor your life with Him and your moral character will be blessed with integrity, your relationships will be blessed with the happiness that comes from fidelity, honesty and trust.

Your purpose in life will be affirmed, your self-esteem made whole.

You will have a solid foundation to relate with those who believe differently.

CATHOLIC PRACTICE – SETTING THIS ANCHOR MORE FIRMLY...

Read a life of Jesus. *Jesus of Nazareth* by Benedict XVI is based on what the Gospels tell us about Jesus. Also read reflections on what Jesus means, a good example is Henri Nouwen's book, *In the Name of Jesus.*

Pray an act of faith often. Affirm and re-affirm your Baptismal calling to be a faithful follower of Jesus Christ. Say **YES** to His invitation to follow Him. Faith is a relationship. Talk to Jesus in prayer, tell Him of your choice for Him, and of your desire to be His disciple.

Choose a Gospel and "walk" through it, noting the words, actions, and feelings of Jesus. What is He saying to you, what is He doing that impresses you, and what is He feeling that inspires you? Receive His words, actions and feelings as blessings. Be determined to take on His mind and heart. Be what your Baptism calls you to, be another Christ bringing the Good News of God's love to the world. Bear the name of Christian humbly and gratefully. Search *"Lectio Divina"*, an enduring tradition.

ON BENDED KNEE...I pray for a deeper relationship with Jesus, the One whom God has sent to show us the way. And so I say to Jesus: open my mind to understand more clearly why God sent You to be my Shepherd, Guide and Savior. Open my heart to embrace Your coming, to welcome You into my daily life, to seek Your companionship through word and sacrament. I love You, Lord Jesus, as brother, friend, and teacher. In times of doubt, help me to remember to say as Thomas the Apostle said: "Yes, Lord, I do believe. Help me in my unbelief." Brother Jesus, be my strength, my inspiration, my guide. Amen.

ANCHOR FIVE
The Eucharist

We are a Eucharistic Church. The Mass is at the center of our
faith tradition. We take Jesus at his word when he said
"This is my body…this is my blood…do this in memory of me."
In this ritual we are fed and transformed and become what we
eat, then we are sent out to bring His love to the world.

THE MASS

We Catholics are a sacramental Church. We see sacrament everywhere, if we look with the eyes of faith. To understand our Catholic faith, we have to know the sacramental principle and appreciate its meaning and application. Simply stated: **A sacrament is a visible sign of God's saving love.** Memorize that line and you will have the key to understanding the heart of your Catholic faith and tradition.

  The Sacramental principle… is deep within our Catholic tradition. Here's how it works. *We see the created universe as sacrament.* When we see God as the Creator of the universe and are moved to express gratitude to God, the earth itself becomes sacramental for us, a visible sign of God's saving love.

  Jesus is Sacrament, a living sign of God's saving love. We read about Him in the Gospels and see how God worked through Him and continues to do so. We read and study His teachings and are inspired by their wisdom and depth, and become aware of God's saving Presence in Him. Jesus is Sacrament. His life, teachings, miracles, suffering, death and resurrection are blessed signs of God's saving Love.

  The Church is sacrament. Over two millennia so far, God's saving Presence has been felt through the Church's preaching of God's message, and its ministries of healing and service to the poor, the sick, the orphaned, the widowed, the uneducated, the imprisoned and so many more. Some days, we are better signs than on other days, true, but still signs of God's saving love, even when broken. You are the Church, together with other believers in Jesus, you are a visible sign of God's love.

  Over time, the Church has identified seven special signs of God's saving love, *the seven sacraments*, each an effective sign of God's saving love in Jesus. In **Baptism** we are born into the Body of Christ on earth and we become children of God, members of the community of believers. In **Confirmation**, we are anointed with the Holy Spirit, sealed into the Mystery of God's saving love. In **Eucharist**, we are nourished and fed with the "daily bread" of God's saving grace, made one with Jesus in sacrifice and sacrament. If we receive **Holy Orders** or **Matrimony** we are called forth from the community to serve the faithful by giving our lives for the building up of God's Reign in the world. **Reconciliation** and **Anointing** are signs of God's love when you and I are in need of healing either because of sin or sickness. The sacraments are seven visible signs of God's saving grace. Unlike ordinary signs which simply point the way to something or give some information, sacramental signs actually do what they signify.

Then there are the *sacramentals*, those visible aids to prayer and spiritual growth that spin off the Sacraments and the sacramental principle. For example, rosary beads being fingered in our hands while we meditate on the major events in Jesus' saving work, holy water at the entrance of church which we take to remind us of our Baptism, a medal bearing a saint's image which reminds us of that saint's virtue, these and many more are sacramentals, visible signs of lesser significance than the seven sacraments, but nevertheless still signs of God's saving love.

Eucharist is the Central Sacrament

In the lived Tradition of the Church, the Eucharist is at the center and heart of sacramental life. The other six sacraments flow from the Eucharist which was given to the Church by Jesus at the Last Supper. "Do this in memory of Me." The grace and blessings that come from all of the sacraments flow from the Good Friday and Easter Sunday action of Jesus. His passion, death and resurrection are one action which the Church calls the Paschal Mystery. And it is into that Mystery that we are initiated through Baptism, Confirmation, and First Communion.

The Mass is the ritual prayer of the Catholic community. It is the community's prayer, therefore not an individual's or even a group's right to change its basic form. It is communal prayer, although personal prayer is essential to its fruitfulness. It is the ritual of the community, shaped by the lived history of the people of God over the centuries, treasured by the community of faith, guarded by the community of faith, universal in its celebration, the action by which Catholics anywhere in the world can be united to Christ and to each other in reverent worship of God.

The night before Jesus died, he commanded his followers to embrace his love, his **REAL PRESENCE** in sacramental form. **"THIS IS MY BODY, TAKE AND EAT. THIS IS MY BLOOD, TAKE AND DRINK. DO THIS IN MEMORY OF ME."** At the heart of the Catholic tradition is the belief in the Real Presence of Jesus in the Eucharist. Other Christian communities believe in Jesus' Presence and may celebrate a ritual of the Last Supper, but none believe as Catholics do, that Jesus is present, body and spirit, soul and divinity, in the celebration of Holy Eucharist. We believe Jesus is truly present under the sacramental sign of the consecrated bread and wine. At every Mass our prayer is: May we become what we eat and drink, a living sign of God's Love in the world.

There is a lot that happens at Mass. Because the Mass is so central to our tradition and faith life, I would like to offer two reflections on the Mass. The first looks at nine different aspects of the Eucharistic celebration any one of which may be the special grace or blessing that you receive on any particular day. The second is a quick walk through the Mass, looking at its sequence and what is happening in each part.

Nine Dimensions of the Mass: what each could mean for you
ONE: RITES

Ritual, song and symbol are capable of touching the human heart in ways that ordinary language does not. At Mass, we stand on the threshold of the Beyond, we reach toward the face of God and let the Spirit of God enter our souls. A rite is a formal ceremony which carries meaning for the community of faith. If it's going to speak to you, you have to *learn the language of ritual.*

For married persons, their wedding ring on the wedding day meant a lot, but add years of companionship through sorrows and joys, the mutual investment of time, talent and treasure and the same ring, though worn and banged up, speaks so much more. To learn the language of ritual, simply search for the deeper meaning. As the Little Prince noted in the book of the same name, what is most precious is what is invisible to the eye.

TWO: COMMUNITY

No one is meant to be alone, even should we feel orphaned, or have no relatives or friends. In Christ we are brothers and sisters. So we go to Mass even when we may not feel like it because our very presence is a blessing to others. While at Mass, take a moment to be consciously aware that you are part of a *family of faith.*

I inquired of an elderly lady one Sunday which part of the Mass she liked most. Her response surprised me. "The sign of peace" she said. Why? "Because that is the only time all week that another human being touches me!" Her community of faith, her Church, was the one family that she could count on for acceptance and warmth. When a child or teenager is the person offering the sign of peace to an elderly person, the impact is doubled! The very presence of youth lifts up the spirit of the elderly.

THREE: GRATITUDE

Eucharist means thanksgiving. At Mass we recall the blessings God has given us. Refusing to be ungrateful, we take time to thank the Source of all our blessings. We come to realize that gratitude is the most basic attitude. *We can never thank God too much. Feel it and say Thank you!*

Gratitude does not come to children and youth naturally. When we are little, our parents may insist that we say thank you but it takes maturation and experience before it comes from a place deeper than our lips. Even so, parents are right in their insistence. It's a healthy antidote to the focus on self that is normal during adolescence, but a focus that eventually must open out to the recognition of one's dependence on others and appreciation for their meaning in our lives. Saying thank you nourishes gratitude in one's heart.

Four: Intimacy

Before Jesus took on our humanity, people feared God and felt distant from their Creator. Jesus changed that. At Mass God comes to us in the simple form of food and drink, in the mysterious Presence of Jesus as the Bread of Love. *God desires an intimate relationship.* Respond to the invitation!

Sharing a meal is one of the most common human experiences of closeness we have. Family meals, banquets celebrating weddings, anniversaries, successes, cooking with others and feasting on the results, not only celebrates the bond that already exists, but also adds to it. Don't' ever underestimate the power that love in the food has to bind people together, especially when feasting with Jesus and His followers at Eucharist!

Five: Strength

Life is not without suffering, disappointment, loss. At Mass we join our pain with the sufferings of Jesus. Jesus does not want us to suffer alone. If no one else is near, He is there to be our companion, to walk with us in good times and bad. With Christ our suffering is redemptive. We are invited to "offer it up", that is, to join our sufferings with the sufferings of Jesus.

Other than wishing for the vigor and energy of youth, few adults relish the thought of having to do adolescence over again! Adolescence can be a difficult and painful time for many young people. Identity issues, career choices, navigating relationships, a maturing sexuality, the prospect of sole responsibility for moral choices, all this and more can add up to some trying times.

Six: Nourishment

The word companion means "bread with us". At Mass we pray as Jesus taught "Give us this day our daily bread." Whatever we might need that day: patience, courage, gentleness, a forgiving heart, wisdom, acceptance and more. *Jesus is your daily bread, in word and sacrament.*

The Blue Zones, written by Dan Buettner, provides a convincing collection of the effects of regular church attendance. He became convinced, after studying actively involved centenarians, that a minimum of monthly church attendance added a certain well-being as well as more years to a person's life. Regular reflection on sacred writings, active participation in a community of faith, and observing a weekly day of prayer and leisure decreased stress, re-charged energy, and made for healthier and happier living.

SEVEN: LOVE

Does God love us? If so, how much? Pondering the crucifix we realize the greatness of God's love for us. Body scourged, head stung with thorns, side pierced by a sword, His body and blood, *His life given for me, for us, for you.* There was nothing more that He could give.

The tiniest words can be the most challenging. Take the word "as" in the command of Jesus that we love one another as He loves us. How did Jesus love? The foundation of his life seems to be His relationship and love for God whom He called "Father." His love was a forgiving love without limits, a love that opened Himself to outcasts and people living on the edge of society, a love that took people as they were and loved them into becoming more, a love that included the sacrifice of life itself.

EIGHT: WISDOM

Do we need support in avoiding evil and making good choices? Of course. At Mass, Sunday after Sunday, we are being built up into a people of sound moral insight and courage. At Mass we are transformed by word and sacrament into the *head, heart, and hands of Jesus, transformed to think, feel, and act like Him.*

Living life can be a challenging journey. As we move through it we are blessed and helped when we receive insights and encouragement from Word and Sacrament. Wisdom is the highest form of knowledge, a knowledge that we need to pray for and seek.

NINE: FOUNDATION

Remember thou keep holy the Sabbath day. Since Sunday was the day Jesus rose from the dead, our Catholic tradition obliges us to participate in the central act of our faith, the Mass. Jesus calls us to and through liturgical prayer. It is here that we receive the wisdom, courage and love to imitate our Lord and Savior. *Keep holy the Lord's Day. Make it your first priority.*

Habit is the better part of virtue. One of the anchors in my life and in the lives of practicing Catholics is the habit of regular Sunday worship. Good habits keep us in solid spiritual shape.

Let's Go to Mass

This will be a short trip through the major parts of the Mass. Spend a few minutes thinking about each part and how it might speak to you.

After the opening greeting, we prepare our hearts for the Eucharist by placing in God's hands any barrier to God's love. Some days we will be carrying the burden of some failure or weakness or sin. So we start with a washing of the soul! Our own, and the sins of humanity. Any sin against oneself or another is a sin against God, a breaking of God's law. Be reconciled and healed. **Lord have mercy, Christ have mercy, Lord have mercy.** God's forgiveness is given. Take and receive.

We go to Mass to be inspired, enlightened, become wiser, gain some light in the darkness. One day we may be baffled about how to handle a relationship that's gone sour, or a decision we have to make. Another day we may be looking for purpose, a new sense of worth and value. Listen intently. Be hungry for God's word. Read along, if possible, as the Scriptures are proclaimed and the homily given. As the Gospel begins, we sign ourselves on our foreheads, lips and heart: **Lord Jesus, may Your word fill my mind, guide my speech and flood my heart.**

We go to Mass to be strengthened in our identity as a follower of Jesus, believing in God as Creator, Redeemer, Sanctifier. **Profess the faith of the community in the creed.**

We go to Mass because we care about the welfare of others and the common good of the world. God answers our prayer initially by the change that takes place in our hearts. Pray the prayers of the community and add your own. **Pray with an open heart.**

We go to Mass so that we can be one with Christ in worshipping God the Creator, and one with His followers in union with the Church. With gratitude we place an offering in the collection basket, doing our part in building up the Body of Christ on this earth. As the bread and wine are brought to the altar, we place ourselves in those elements. As they are soon to be transformed into the Love of Christ, we pray that we, too, may be transformed, thinking as Jesus did, and loving as He loved. **An offering of self.**

We go to Mass to offer to God the most perfect sacrifice of all time, namely, Jesus on the cross. **The consecration** and **Eucharistic prayer** are in direct response to the command of Jesus to **do this in memory of Me.**

We go to Mass so that we may profess our faith in God as our Creator Parent, praying the prayer that Jesus taught us, calling God Abba, daddy, Father. God is not distant and impersonal, but close and personal. If God is the source of our existence and Jesus encourages us to call God "Father", then we become brothers and sisters to each other. **Be in solidarity with others, with God, with all creation.**

We go to Mass to be fed by the love of Jesus: a love that is forgiving, a love that is reverent, a love that seeks the best for the other, a love that is gentle, a love that is genuine, a love that is committed. **Communion** means **union with God and the community of believers.**

We are blessed and invited to **go in peace to love and serve God and one another.** As Jesus has become Bread for the world, for us, so we are sent to become bread for the world, for others.

HOW TO "GET SOMETHING OUT OF MASS"

Active participation is the key to "getting something out of the Mass." It is not a spectator sport or entertainment or something to be done by a pastor and parishioners who pray and sing hymns. The more you get involved and actually participate, the more you will get from it. Participation means **do your parts.** The words of the hymns are meant to feed your soul. If you don't like to sing, then look for what God is saying to you in the lyrics. Respond with enthusiasm and investment of spirit for all the people's parts. Say the Creed from memory! Always bring a contribution to church with you so you can add your part to the community's collection. Remember the widow in the Gospel who gave, not from her excess, but from her needs. Your contribution helps pay the light and heat bills, wages for staff, and all the programs of education, social out-reach to the needy, works of justice and peace, and more.

If you want to get something out of life, you have to show up! A team doesn't become a team if no one shows up for practice! Organizations of every type and kind are built into something good by those who show up, the attenders, the active participants! It's the people who show up at the meetings that run the world, someone once told me. It's true.

The old adages are also true: if you want something out of Liturgy, you have to put something into it. You get what you give. Life is not free. No sweat, no gain. Believe me: these sayings are true about our relationship with God. Like any other relationship -- a friendship, a family circle, a team experience – we have to "show up," that is, be present and positive, if something good is to happen, if we are to get something out of it. Liturgy is ritual, ritual is like poetry. One has to look deeper to find the treasure but it is usually worth the effort.

The Obligation of Sunday Mass

Going back to the time of Moses, over one thousand years before Jesus was born, our Jewish sisters and brothers kept holy the Sabbath, the Lord's Day. On the Lord's Day they pondered the Holy Scriptures, offered praise and worship to God, and spent the rest of the day in leisure. For Catholics, active participation in Sunday Mass is essential to growing in spirituality. As with any other human activity –sports, family meals, life at home, friendship –we can view the action from the sidelines or we can genuinely get with the program and participate. When we do participate, not only we but the whole community reaps the benefits.

Young Catholics who give high priority to Sunday Eucharist, who have the courage and moral strength to participate at Mass even when their parents might not, are a blessing to the world. Keep holy the Lord's Day. When that is in proper order, the rest of life falls into place. Thank God for the courage Catholics have to be counter cultural, who do the right thing because it is the right thing to do: give Sunday Eucharist and worship of God in the community of faith top priority.

Suggestions for a fruitful observance of the Lord's Day:

- Develop the habit of making Sunday different from the rest of the week. Think of it as the time for you to connect with the deepest part of yourself, with the rich companionship of family and friends, and with your God who is the source of your life and your capacity to love.

- Go on-line to find the readings for the Sunday liturgy and read them over looking for what God might be saying to you that day.

- Get to church 10 or 15 minutes before Mass, be a part of the hospitality ministry and greet others. If your church is not particularly hospitable, that should not stop you from being friendly. Let God's love work through you to brighten up someone else's day.

- Pick up a hymbook or litergical aide, check out the lyrics chosen for the day, and look for God's message there. Your "daily bread," your inspiration for the week, may well be hidden in the music. Don't let it slip by you.

- Make the rest of the day one of leisure and rest. Take the initiative to visit relatives, neighbors, friends, or look forward to meeting someone new whom God might well be placing in your life that day.

The Sunday experience has changed dramatically since I was young. Then all businesses were closed. So were the stores, so shopping was not a Sunday activity like it is today. Sunday worship was given a priority over school events and organized sports. The vast majority of Americans attended their church services. When I was in high school 75-85% of Catholics attended Mass every weekend. Sadly, today the average is about 35%. A wonderful challenge for you who are young Catholics today is be the generation that renews our society and the world by becoming practicing Catholics. When I was an adolescent, it was part of the tenor of the times for Catholics to strive to be "good Catholics", that is, seriously committed to know our Faith and to practice it faithfully.

THIS ANCHOR OF EUCHARIST WILL...

Transform your mind into the mind and heart of Jesus.

Keep you grounded in the humble truth of God's sovereignty and your dependence on God.

Help you live "green," that is, have a genuine reverence for the environment and all that God has made.

Open your eyes to see life and the world as God sees it.

Open your heart to sincere gratitude, the most basic attitude in life.

Raise your self-esteem as a child of God, invited to intimacy with God in Jesus.

Foster your spiritual growth within the community of believers.

Integrate your moral desires with your Christian moral core.

Lead you to see your faults and difficulties as vehicles of God's grace.

Help you build your priorities on rock not on sand.

CATHOLIC PRACTICE – SETTING THIS ANCHOR MORE FIRMLY...

Show up! Be present to others. Lead by your example. Foster community in Jesus' name.

Love the Mass. Let it feed your spirit as only ritual can. Accept Jesus as God's gift to you and to humanity. Live the Mass and you will live your Faith and bless the world.

Resolve to actively participate at Mass every Sunday and Holy Day. Volunteer for a ministry: server, lector, Extraordinary Minister of Holy Communion, usher, greeter.

Fast from food and drink, (except water) for one hour before Mass out of reverence and in preparation for reception of Holy Communion.

Genuflect or bow as an act of reverence toward the Blessed Sacrament whenever entering or leaving chapel or church, and whenever crossing in front of the reserved Eucharist in the Tabernacle.

Invest in a prayer book that has all the readings and Mass prayers.

Memorize the people's parts of the Mass, such as the Confiteor (I confess), Gloria and Creed.

At Mass, remember to look beyond the visible bread and wine to the love of God in Jesus that this Sacrament contains. See with the eyes of faith all the love God has for you, especially evident in the passion, death, and resurrection of Jesus.

ON BENDED KNEE... Lord Jesus, I believe You are the One whom God has sent to show us the way. Open my heart to Your Presence in the Eucharist. Open my eyes to see with the eyes of faith how much You love me. Open my mouth in gratitude to You for blessing me and the whole wide world with the Sacrament of the Mass. No matter where I might go on this earth, You are there to comfort me and give me strength. Accept my gratitude and let me rest in You with confidence and trust. Amen.

ANCHOR SIX
Reverence for Life and All Creation

From the moment of conception to the point of
natural death we carry a profound respect for human life,
a respect that translates into a reverence for all of
God's creation. At its most basic level,
we are environmentalists, seeking to know
God's purpose for Creation and respecting the same.

The Environment

Water is essential to life. Most Americans probably take the availability of safe water for granted. I know I did, having every reason to think the supply was safe and inexhaustible. Reality struck on my third canoe trip into the Canadian Boundary waters. During my first trip, in 1954, water was safe to take and drink right out of the lakes. By my third, acid rain had polluted the region and canoeists were warned not to drink lake water without purifying it. How could hundreds of square miles of pure wilderness, with its countless lakes and streams, pristine from time immemorial, be taken away from humanity?

Since that time I have witnessed scarcity of water, polluted or pure, elsewhere. In Kenya, Africa, traveling there with a group of students and teachers in 2009, I felt the anxiety of Kenyan families whose daily trek for water resulted in jugs from polluted streams. The only water safe for drinking and cooking was costly bottled water. Water for bathing and household chores had to come from gutters and tanks they constructed to catch rain from their rooftops. Showers and baths were rare for the Kenyans we visited, a reality we quickly learned to appreciate.

Water is perhaps the most important natural resource that is endangered for future generations, but not the only one. Farmland, air, vegetation, animal life, and rain forests are also endangered by the pollutants which are spoiling our environment. Working to safeguard the environment is a moral imperative, according to Catholic teaching.

John Paul II, highlighted the negative implications for the world's impoverished people caused by "the worsening of the ecological question." He underscored the fact that it is the poor who feel most harshly the effects of pollution and environmental disasters. Pope Francis, from the very begining of his papacy, called all people to respect the environment. In his homily at his inauguration Mass which took place on the Feast of St. Joseph whose mission was one of protection, the new Pope urged Catholics and the entire world to protect the environment. He chose the name Francis after St. Francis of Assisi who lived among the poor, choosing to live simply, but also the saint who is loved even by people of no religious faith because of his profound love of nature and the animal world. Along with Popes John Paul and Benedict, our U.S Catholic Bishops have urged Catholics to get involved, not only in cleaning up the environment but also by providing solutions to world hunger and the wide range of ecological challenges.

Basic Catholic doctrine teaches that the created world is God's, first and foremost, not humanity's. The earth and all its parts have been given to us to use, not abuse. And our use of it is not absolute, that is, we are subject to a moral order that commands respect for all of God's creation. With one billion members scattered across the globe, the Catholic Church takes environmental issues seriously and encourages its members to get involved. Beginning with first principles, namely, that all of creation belongs to God, that all creation is good, and that God has entrusted to humanity the awesome responsibility of being its stewards, our Church sticks to its principles with a stubbornness that is enviable.

Beautiful things are happening as more and more people get on the bandwagon of environmental concern. Recycling, humane treatment of animals, composting, organic gardening and farming, the search for alternative forms of energy, conservation efforts of all types, and making our sidewalks and buildings more accessible –these efforts which may have begun as movements are becoming institutionalized, at least in the developed nations. When a person of faith sees the environment from the eyes of faith, that is, sees all of creation as gift from a loving God, the motivation to have reverence for persons and things is strengthened.

Some social scientists and others who study demographics, climate change, and economic conditions around the globe suggest that humanity may be reaching a point of no return. Either we clean up our act or our actions will clean us up! The effects of industrialization, as much as they have benefitted our lifestyles and brought comfort for a minority of the human race, the majority living in undeveloped nations seem to be paying the price. These issues are extremely complicated and our Church must contribute what it can to resolve them. No easy task, and one that requires peoples the globe over to work together. Our Church, already a global community and perhaps the only organization to be truly global at the grass root level is poised to become even more of an instrument of healing and hope in the coming decades.

Catholic Church, a Rare Vessel

I was struck by an article in the Minneapolis *Star Tribune* (4/23/08) at the time Pope Benedict visited the United States. The author, Michael Gerson, noted that the Catholic Church has endured attacks from without and within, and has 'remained an indispensable institution for several reasons." First, it defends reason against the "dictatorship of relativism." The Church affirms that human reason can arrive at objective truths and that humanity is not served well by the belief that subjectivity alone, that is, a kind of "whateverism," that everyone's personal belief, is absolutely true.

When "whatever" is the response you give or get in a conversation, checking it out may be a good idea. Is the topic or action being discussed a matter of opinion or a matter of fact? It has been popular in recent years for many people to treat opinion as fact, or any opinion as valuable as any other as if truth doesn't matter, and it does. An opinion may be false or dangerous, others quite harmless. The author's observation about the Catholic Church is that its insistence that there are objective truths, that not everything is relative, provides a necessary guide to humanity for its own sake.

Second, Gerson continues, the Church defends human dignity against secularism and materialism. Pope John Paul II warns: "The criterion of personal dignity is replaced by the criterion of efficiency, functionality and usefulness: others are considered not for what they are but for what they have, do, and produce. This is the supremacy of the strong over the weak." Gerson praises Catholicism for being the main defender of human dignity, applying this belief with remarkable consistency –to the unborn and the elderly, the immigrant and the disabled. The author continued:

> *"An institution accused of being superstition (sic) is now the world's most steadfast defender of rationality and human rights. It remains a rare vessel entrusted with an exceptional wisdom born from suffering and experience that just might save humanity from itself."*

The values deeply held within Catholicism are critical to the welfare of the human race. When the Church pushes political agendas, it invites criticism from those who, mistakenly, believe that religion and politics, morality and public policy, should always be separated. The fact of the matter is that many political issues have significant moral content, and the religious institutions which cherish human values have every right and obligation to get involved and make their voices heard.

Our Church is one of those institutions that contributes officially to the discussion and development of legislation on both the national and state levels. In Minnesota, we do it through two organizations: the National Conference of Catholic Bishops and the Minnesota Catholic Conference.

THE NATIONAL CONFERENCE OF CATHOLIC BISHOPS with headquarters in Washington, D.C., promotes legislation and programs that favor human life at all stages. Their advocacy includes protection of the unborn, abolition of the death penalty, assistance to the elderly and disadvantaged, economic justice, preferential option for the poor, war and peace, immigration, education, and other critical issues as they arise. The leadership and staff of the NCCB make it their mission to promote human and Christian values in the development and implementation of the law of the land.

Locally, the **MINNESOTA CONFERENCE OF BISHOPS,** is the voice of the Church for legislation and programs at the state level. Its agenda includes: finding solutions to poverty, promoting economic justice, respecting human rights in pro-life issues, and assisting legislators in the development of policies and laws regarding education, criminal justice, immigration, marriage, and more. The voice of the faith community must be heard in the political process since most political issues have a moral component and affect the common good of society.

From Conception to Natural Death

The Catholic Church's commitment to the sacredness of life from the moment of conception to natural death is unconditional. The Church's position is pro-life all the way. To that end, Catholics strongly oppose abortion, euthanasia and the death penalty, and anything in between which violates human dignity and a person's right to life.

Our Church is active in promoting legislation which is pro-life both at the national level and at the state level. Catholics from various parishes participate in protests at places where abortions are administered, giving public witness to the evil of abortion as they offer encouragement to women seeking abortions to reconsider.

Assistance is available through agencies such as the **TOTAL LIFE CARE CENTERS** –26 of them in Minnesota and Wisconsin—where women with unplanned pregnancies can receive assistance with physical, emotional, and social needs. **THE SETON CENTERS** in St. Paul and Minneapolis offer medical and social services for pregnant single women and for low-income couples. Their programs include pregnancy testing, foster care, adoption and post-adoption services, parenting education and children's services, support groups, and counseling to individuals and families.

Some years ago I was asked to show up at a hospital delivery room in case the child to be born needed an emergency Baptism. Preliminary tests had shown that, due to a rare genetic abnormality, the baby to be born could be severely malformed, and if he survived, would have permanent and serious limitations. One medical professional had encouraged an abortion. But the pregnant teen and her family met, and chose to give birth, willing to accept the consequences of their decision. When Jake was born he looked quite normal but it soon became obvious that his hearing, vision, speech, and mobility would be severely impaired. The family surrounded this child with love and, in return, has received from him a great measure of joy. Years later, at his mom's wedding, Jake was in the wedding party, wheelchair bound, suited in a tux, and wearing a toothy smile!

As individuals mature so do societies. One of the great advances in modern times is the movement that has brought intellectually and physically challenged persons out of the shadows and into the full light of normal life. It is, I suppose, a natural response to apply a label to differently challenged people and exclude them from our regular social networks. I had not had much personal experience living with and working with persons with disabilities and then I met John. This was more than 40 years ago.

> The event was a Catholic youth rally at the St. Paul civic center which drew some 3,000 high school teens. A day long program of workshops and seminars ended with a square dance in which all three thousand young people participated. It was new for me to see a group of teens treating this intellectually challenged teenager as one of them. No special treatment, no explanations needed or given, just include John like everyone else. At that same event, a group of forty hearing impaired teens led the huge crowd of thousands in a song through sign language. Again, challenged kids doing what any kid will do: having fun with others their age.
>
> A brief encounter with John taught me to *see the person, not the handicap*. Witnessing teens whose hearing was severely impaired behaving like any other teen taught me to see the persons not the impairment. That was and is the secret. See the person, not the limitation! What a difference this has made ever since.

For the most part, people can take care of themselves for most of their lives. But many people find themselves in situations that require assistance. I wrote an historical thesis years ago on the Good Shepherd Sisters in St. Paul. They had come to Minnesota in 1868 at the request of the young Father John Ireland. Back then, St. Paul was a frontier town with a number of girls and women unable to fend for themselves. The Sisters provided a safe residence and an education for them until they were able to get jobs and move on in life. The youngest resident on record they ever took in was a newborn left on their doorstep, while the oldest was a lady in her seventies who had trouble staying sober.

TWO NAMES EVERY CATHOLIC SHOULD KNOW

JEAN VANIER and **HENRI NOUWEN.** Feeling called to a life of assisting the developmentally disabled, Vanier resigned his naval commission with the British navy and began to establish homes where developmentally disabled could live together with volunteers and staff. In 1964, naming his first home L'Arche, a French word meaning Noah's ark, Vanier launched a lifetime of learning from the disabled. His movement spread and in 1969, he established the first L'Arche in the North America.

It was there, near Toronto, that Henri Nouwen chose to live. Nouwen, a renowned priest, psychologist, author, and professor, left the intellectual atmosphere of Harvard and Yale for the simplicity of the L'Arche community. His books, especially *The Road to Daybreak,* and *Adam, God's Beloved,* are powerful expressions of how friendship with the developmentally disabled can transform one's life. There are more than 130 L'Arche communities around the world, each one having a profound impact not only on the residents of the communities but also on all who come in contact with the movement. Vanier's invitation to befriend the disabled and Nouwen's exposition of the gifts they offer to society, are making the world a better place.

The Gospel as lived by Catholics worldwide has inspired the establishment of countless institutions and movements that promote human life. The works of compassion, education, health services, ministries to variously challenged individuals, seeking justice and peace, --all these and more are responses to the Christian vocation to have reverence for human life and all of God's creation.

Recent legislation in a few States has made euthanasia legal. This question of end-of-life morality is likely to loom larger as the movement expands to hasten death when a terminal condition exists. It can seem so reasonable. But the Catholic position is consistently pro-life. Under no circumstances is assisted suicide permissible. Life is God's gift and no one has the right to take life, either one's own or another's. And so, under the sponsorship of the Church many ministries to the sick, the dying, and elderly give witness to this pro-life position. All across the globe, Catholic homes for the elderly, nursing homes, and homes for the dying are doing wonderful work. Of the many in the Twin Cities area, two are noted here.

Located near Cleveland Avenue and Interstate 94, Our Lady of Good Counsel Free Cancer Home was established by the **DOMINICAN SISTERS OF THE SICK POOR**. Their specialized ministry in their Cancer Homes is to provide hospice care to people in their final struggle with cancer, regardless of age, race, creed or color. This religious Order was begun by Mary Walsh, a poor Irish immigrant who settled in New York City and discovered her life's work of charity and compassion.

A chance (or was it Providential?) experience that she had with a desperately sick and poor mother one day led her to quit her job so she could devote all her time and energy to help this woman. She began to work full time, locating the dying poor, giving them a dignified home to live out their final days. Anyone who has had a relative or friend at Good Counsel Home has seen the wonderful work of this religious Order and felt the warm love of God in the environment and personnel of the Home. It is a great place to spend one's closing days. (In 2009, this ministry was transferred to the Franciscan Health Community.)

Another ministry in the Twin Cities which serves the elderly poor is the Holy Family Residence operated by the **LITTLE SISTERS OF THE POOR**. Located near 7th street just a few blocks from the Excel Center in St. Paul, this facility has apartments for assisted living as well as a fully staffed nursing home. This ministry serves people who do not have the financial resources to live in nursing homes and who have no family with whom they might live. Described by some as the "Cadillac" of nursing homes, Holy Family Residence is a great place to prepare for one's crossing over to the "other side".

THIS ANCHOR, REVERENCE FOR LIFE AND ALL CREATION WILL...

Help you avoid the life and death decisions that, if immoral, could burden your peace of mind the rest of your life.

Strengthen your resolve and actions to protect human life from conception to natural death.

Make it easier to always choose life.

Give you the courage and emotional strength needed when you are responsible for the well-being of others, be they infants, children, elderly parents and grandparents, dependent adults, or the disadvantaged.

Help you see the person and not the handicap or limitation.

CATHOLIC PRACTICE - SETTING THIS ANCHOR MORE FIRMLY...

Take your right to vote seriously by studying the positions of the candidates and weighing the issues for and against moral and pro-life values.

Support the Pro-life movement by donating funds and goods to Life Care centers, participating in Pro-Life gatherings.

Volunteer at nursing homes, visit the elderly in your family and neighborhood, beginning with grandparents, uncles and aunts.

Work as a volunteer with Special Olympics, promote accessibility wherever you can.

Become an avid recycler, compost your garbage, get involved in cleaning up your environment, be "green" conscious with fertilizers and other chemicals.

Simplify your life by moving along to free stores and other distribution centers the unused clothing and other items you do not need.

ON BENDED KNEE...Jesus, Lord of my life. Deepen within my heart an appreciation for the gift of life. Let me treat every person with dignity, regardless of physical, mental, spiritual or moral limitations. Let me see with the eyes of faith your Presence in others. Give me wisdom in my relationships, courage in my actions, moral conviction in my choices. May this anchor of reverence for life become more and more a part of my moral character so that, when and if confronted by the choice, I will always choose life. Amen.

ANCHOR SEVEN
Respect for the Mind

Our Church has a remarkable reverence for the human intellect. Throughout our history we have struggled to understand and to teach. We believe in science *and* faith, not science versus faith. Our commitment to education at all levels has contributed immensely to the progress of the human race from monastic institutions begun in earlier centuries to Third World elementary schools today.

SCIENCE AND FAITH

The history of the human race records quite a wrestling match between faith and science, between faith and reason. At times, faith led the way, not always correctly. At times, reason led with the same mixed results. Faith tends to supply answers to questions that reason or science either can't or can't yet answer. Before science arrived at the fact that the earth was round, faith taught that it was flat. After a while, faith accepted the truth of science. The knowledge gap had been filled. Science answered the questions over time, presenting a plausible response to questions about when our world began and how it developed. Little doubt that these are questions for science to answer.

On the other side, science does not answer the question of Who created the world and why. Those are faith questions. So are these: Is Jesus truly human and divine? Is there an afterlife? Does God know our names and care about us? Is the Church inspired by the Holy Spirit of God? Was Mary conceived without sin? Is Jesus present in the consecrated Eucharist? Does God hear and answer our prayers? Does God speak through other world religions? These and many others like them are faith questions with faith answers. Reason can play a part in coming to the answers but basically some questions are solely in the realm of faith.

FRANCIS S. COLLINS is one of the most noted scientists of our modern era. He was raised in a household that was neutral toward religion. As he grew through college and his graduate studies he claimed, for a while, to be an agnostic, one who believed that, if there is a God, that God can't be known. Then he became an atheist, denying the very existence of God. One day he found himself discussing religious belief with a Methodist minister who suggested he read C.S. Lewis' *Mere Christianity* In Lewis, himself an atheist turned Christian, Collins found answers to God's existence even before he could articulate the question. Collin's search for God led him to the God of Abraham, Moses, and Jesus and to a commitment to Jesus Christ.

As the young Collins moved along in his career, mathematics and physics was his first choice but for reasons he never quite grasped he found himself pursuing biology and medicine, culminating in a degree in medicine. Little did he know then that he would become the director of the Genome Project, one of the most ground-breaking scientific discoveries of modern times. The Genome Project resulted in decoding the DNA for humans, the construction book of humanity that, up until now, only God had known. This code comprises more than three billion letters, which, if written on 8 by 11 inch paper, filling each sheet then stacking them on top of each other, the pile would be as high as the Washington monument!

In his book, *The language of God*, Collins makes the case for science *and* faith. The more one knows about science and the factual evidence of our complex universe, the more the case for the existence of God is built. Collins has been there –an agnostic and an atheist. He concludes that both positions are weak. Agnostics may well be avoiding the task of rational pursuit of the question, feeling safe in the "I don't want to know" body of believers. Atheists may well be blinded by bias against religion, or choose not to pursue the question of God's existence beyond their chosen stopping point, or refusal to accept the possibility that there are some questions that science simply can't answer but faith can.

Not all Christian denominations have accepted the theory of **evolution**. The Catholic Church, perhaps most assuredly so in the remarks of Pope John Paul II, not only accepts the theory but, as the Pope stated, accepts it beyond an "hypothesis." The Catholic Church sees no conflict between the theory of evolution and the Catholic faith. Why could God not design a universe that unfolds in evolutionary fashion? What an amazing accomplishment! What John Paul posits as the foundational truth underpinning evolution is that there is One God, not several, who is the Source of the creation we know and love. The universe did not happen by chance, or fall into place without a supreme Intelligence guiding it. God Is! And God created the universe.

Catholic Scientists

If you were to search "Catholic Priest Scientists" one name that will appear is **FR. GEORGE LE- MAITRE**, a Belgian Roman Catholic priest physicist who is credited with proposing a theory about the origins of the universe that later became known as the Big Bang Theory. This theory opened up the exploration of an expanding universe. Albert Einstein was a participant at the convention of scientists in San Francisco in 1927 when LeMaitre presented his theory. Einstein was impressed and stated so. If you look up LeMaitre on the internet you can locate a photo of LeMaitre and Einstein together at that conference. The Catholic Church has long been interested in the expanded universe. The Vatican Observatory is one of the oldest astronomical institutions in the world.

In the course of centuries many discoveries and developments in the sciences were made by Catholics, world famous for their contributions. The presence of women is notably lacking which is not so much a commentary on the Church as it is on the cultural and historical developments of the past. For centuries, women held home and family together while men were expected to succeed in the marketplace and economy. Some of the more famous Catholic scientists are:

- Leonardo DaVinci - artist and sculptor, paleontologist, evolutionary biologist, astronomer, geographer, geologist

- Galileo Galilei - physicist, mathematician, astronomer

- Enrico Fermi - physicist, developer of nuclear reactor

- Gregor Mendel (monk) - geneticist

- Louis Pasteur - chemist and inventor of Pasteurization

- Nicholas Copernicus (priest) - first to propose that the earth revolved around the sun

- Alexander Fleming - inventor of penicillin

- Saint Albert the Great - Patron of scientists, medieval authority on physics, geography, astronomy, mineralogy, chemistry, zoology, and physiology

- Johann Muller (Bishop) - astronomer

- Luigi Galvani - father of electricity

- Guglielmo Marconi - father of radio

The relationship between Galileo and the Catholic Church is a prime example of the wrestling match between faith and science. Galileo has been called the "Father of Modern Science" by Albert Einstein. He was ahead of his time and found himself in dispute with some other scientists and Church authorities about whether the earth revolved around the sun or the sun around the earth (which had been the dominant belief and theory.) Eventually science proved that Galileo was right and faith submitted to science. It wasn't until 1992, that the Church under Pope John Paul II expressed regret on how it handled the Galileo affair. Why so long? An embarrassment to us Catholics, for sure, and an example of the saying that Rome (meaning the Catholic Church) moves slowly, a characteristic of institutions generally. But we Catholics accept our failure in this and hope to improve in the future.

Commitment to Education Over the Centuries

One of the major contributions of the Catholic Church in its earlier centuries was that made by monks who preserved much of the Greek and Roman classics for future generations. They opened schools and eventually established the first universities in the Western world. In Medieval Europe, the Catholic Church was the first to establish universities, often from schools that had been established earlier as cathedral schools.

Closer to our time is the massive contribution made by the teaching orders of religious brothers and sisters who, here in the U.S. and elsewhere, conducted elementary, secondary, collegiate and graduate levels of education. The Catholic Church has a remarkable record of achievement all along the educational spectrum, from the cradle to the grave.

The development of the teaching orders of Catholic men and women is a phenomenon in itself. Realizing that a human mind is a terrible thing to waste, and inspired by the Christian Gospel, thousands of Catholic adults (usually young) joined religious communities whose mission was to teach. By their willingness to live in community with only the bare necessities of life, and promising to live as celibates (a wise and necessary requirement in community life), they committed themselves to obey the Rule of their Order and pursue the mission of their community. Usually after a trial period experiencing the life and work of their chosen Order, they would take vows of poverty, chastity and obedience.

When I was in grade school (1942-1950), several School Sisters of Notre Dame lived in the convent next door to our family home. Their salary was $1, one dollar, a day each, which was pooled into the community coffers that paid for their food, clothing and personal needs. My tuition in first grade was 50 cents a month. By the time I graduated eighth grade it had gone up to $1 a month, ten dollars a year. With the combination of the contributed services of the Sisters (simplicity of life and no personal salary) and the volunteering and financial support of parish members the children of working class families were able to receive an excellent education and move on to secondary school and higher education.

Catholics in the United States, currently among the wealthiest and most educated in the country, can trace their rise largely to the generosity and sacrifice of the women and men who dedicated their energies and hearts to the mission of Catholic Education. As the members of Religious Orders dedicated to education contributed greatly to the improvement of the quality of life for millions of Americans, this same phenomenon is happening in Third World countries now.

At the time of this writing, I am serving as Chaplain at Cretin-Derham Hall high school. This school has two religious orders, the Sisters of St. Joseph of Carondolet and the Christian Brothers, as its founding Orders, both committed to education, religious and secular, since their beginnings more than three hundred years ago.

THE SISTERS OF ST. JOSEPH OF CARONDOLET

The Sisters of St. Joseph of Carondolet were founded by a group of women in France and soon expanded into missions in the United States. The first Sisters arrived in Minnesota in 1851 to teach the children of Irish, German and Italian immigrants at the Cathedral school. Later they founded St. Joseph's Academy, the first school for girls in the great northwest. In 1854, when the cholera epidemic hit St. Paul, the Sisters cared for its victims at their newly established St. Joseph's hospital. Thus began exceptionally effective ministries in education and medicine which continue today. The Sisters established a second high school in St. Paul, Derham Hall, on the campus of the College of St. Catherine, and three high schools in Minneapolis, St. Margaret's Academy, Holy Angels Academy, and St. Anthony School. The CSJ's as they are called, were joined by other congregations of women religious, whose contribution to the Church and society in the upper Midwest is incalculable.

In recent years, with a decline in membership, the Sisters of St. Joseph initiated the Consociates, women who commit themselves to the ministries of their Order. The CSJ's currently number 12,200 Sisters and 4,500 Consociates throughout the world.

Since their arrival in the Twin Cities, the Sisters of St. Joseph have operated four high schools and dozens of grade schools in the Twin Cities and beyond. Besides Derham Hall in the current Cretin-Derham Hall merged school, their most enduring institution is Saint Catherine University, which in 2009 had an enrollment of just more than five thousand students in their college and graduate programs. For over a hundred and fifty years, the CSJ's have provided quality education and health care in Minnesota.

THE BROTHERS OF THE CHRISTIAN SCHOOLS

The Brothers of the Christian Schools. John Baptist DeLaSalle was a wealthy and learned Frenchman who was inspired by his Catholic faith to open schools for boys living in poverty. He developed strategies for teaching that were revolutionary at the time and he attracted other young men to join him in his mission. He chose the title of Brothers because he wanted his teachers to live in community as brothers and to treat as brothers the boys they educated. Founded in 1680, DeLaSalle's community of Brothers experienced gradual growth and by 1810, numbered 160 brothers teaching in France and Italy. By 1900, there were 14,631 Brothers teaching in 35 countries.

The Christian Brothers came to St. Paul in 1871 to teach the boys at Cathedral grade school, working jointly with the Sisters of St. Joseph who had been teaching both boys and girls since 1851. The Brothers' ministry quickly evolved into the establishment of Cretin High School. In later years the Brothers established other schools in the Twin Cities, notably DeLaSalle, Hill, Brady, Grace, and Benilde.

As the Christian Brothers had a profound influence in educating Catholic boys here in the Twin Cities, they are now growing in numbers and building schools in Africa among the poorest of the poor. Brother Dominic Ehrmantraut (a graduate of Cretin High School) with other Brothers from the United States have established a Scholasticate in Nairobi, Kenya, where African Catholic men prepare to become Brothers, intending to teach in their mission schools in South Africa, Ethiopia, Uganda, Eritrea and Kenya. As the numbers of Brothers is diminishing in the U.S. the charism of John Baptist de LaSalle continues to expand with impressive numbers of laity choosing to become LaSallian Associates.

The Sisters of St. Joseph of Carondolet and the DeLaSalle Christian Brothers are only two of many congregations of women and men who have advanced education here and abroad. The Church is growing quickly in Third World countries like Kenya where religious Orders, old and new, are building schools, at times against all odds, to bring the Gospel and basic education to anxious learners. On my first trip to Kenya in 1995, I visited Catholic schools in the slums of Nairobi and saw first hand the enormous good that is being accomplished under Catholic sponsorship.

A newly formed Catholic religious order serving the poor in Africa is the **CONGREGATION OF BROTHERS OF ST. CHARLES LWANGA**. I witnessed their work with street kids in the slums of Nairobi, in their trade and technical schools for boys, and in their residences for homeless boys. Given their mission, besides providing educational opportunities to homeless children, they also provide food, shelter, clothing, and medical attention to thousands of marginalized children and youth.

INSTITUTIONAL STRENGTH

One of the beauties of a weathered, global and stable institution like our Church is that when needs arise in one part of the world, those with wealth and means in other parts can be linked to meet some of those needs. With missions already established in thousands of poverty areas around the globe, when earthquakes, tsunamis, hurricanes, and other natural disasters strike, the Catholic Church is there to offer help, able to garner financial and personnel assistance from Catholic Charities, Caritas International, and from thousands of parishes spread worldwide.

Besides the Church's ministry to its members in their local parishes, its next largest ministry is in education. Convinced that progress and genuine development of peoples anywhere on this globe depends on quality education, the Church is relentless in its efforts to teach everyone, especially those who are poor.

THIS ANCHOR OF RESPECT FOR THE MIND WILL...

Insure that you appreciate the contributions that Catholics make toward education at all levels from pre-school to graduate education.

Provide basic elements when you discuss science and religion, reason and faith.

Affirm your conviction that a human mind is a terrible gift to waste.

Help you maintain a healthy respect for the human intellect, its capacity and the responsibility to use it to fulfill God's purpose for the common good of humanity.

CATHOLIC PRACTICE - SETTING THIS ANCHOR MORE FIRMLY...

Support Catholic education however you can.

Volunteer to tutor at one of the Catholic schools in the inner city.

Go on-line to keep in touch with the goals and efforts of the Minnesota Catholic Conference relative to legislative issues and the need for Catholic involvement.

Appreciate the sacrifice and commitment of our predecessors who built the Catholic educational system and continue it today.

Become a Sister or Brother and carry on the worthy mission of the Religious Orders

ON BENDED KNEE...O God of generous love. Thank You for the spirit of generosity that inspired and continues to inspire thousands of young men and women to commit their energies and talents to education. Bless those upon whose shoulders we stand, grateful, and bless those who will choose this noble vocation in the future, hopeful. The challenges they face are sometimes overwhelming. May they be strengthened each day by your Spirit and by our prayers. Their work builds Your Reign of justice, good will, and peace upon our earth. Amen.

Anchor Eight
Easter People

We are an Easter people and Alleluia is our song!
Death is not the end but rather a transformation into eternal
life. Those who have gone before us with the sign of faith
remain joined to us in a Communion of Saints.

THE LITURGICAL YEAR

One of the treasures of our Faith is the Liturgical year. Updated every so many centuries, the Liturgical calendar invites us into God's Mysterious Presence in Jesus. In the Liturgy, we celebrate the significant events of the history of our people, and we celebrate some of the significant people of our history. The Liturgical Year begins with the birth of Jesus (Advent and Christmas), and continues through His death and resurrection (Lent and Easter). Around these two major festivities, we celebrate what is called Ordinary Time. The Liturgical Year is our most basic religion book because our liturgy is a primary source of what we believe. It is the well which feeds our faith, the well spring of grace which energizes us to practice it.

I have found it effective to follow this simple practice. Every time I participate in a liturgy, I consciously try to look for the "bread," the nourishment for my soul that is in that liturgy. For example, every saint's feast day highlights an aspect of the unique spiritual flavor of that saint. St. Francis of Assisi (October 4) moves me to live more simply and make his prayer for peace more manifest in my daily life. St. Katherine Drexel (March 3) moves me to support Risen Christ, an inner city Catholic school. The list of feasts and saints days is long and beautiful, the "bread" supply is endless. No liturgy is boring when you come to it hungry. (Reminds me of the Italian saying about food: the best recipe is hunger! Same saying applies when considering food for the soul.)

Although Christmas may seem bigger because of the traditions that surround it and the hold it has on the imagination of our culture, for Catholics Easter is the most important. The Resurrection of Jesus from the dead and the promise of eternal life are two of God's greatest gifts to humanity. The celebration of Holy Week, with its liturgies on Holy Thursday, Good Friday, and the Easter vigil, is the highlight of the year for Catholics. Those who take these days seriously and participate in these liturgies participate in the Mystery of God's saving presence in beautiful and powerful ways.

Holy Week: the Triduum

HOLY THURSDAY commemorates the Last Supper when Jesus washed the feet of his disciples, expecting them to serve one another with love and a generous heart. Jesus had taught them: "I have not come to be served but to serve," and said, "As I have done, so must you do for each other", that is, serve one another! Holy Thursday also celebrates the institution of the Holy Eucharist, the central sacrament of our faith. "Do this in memory of Me." It is a great grace and blessing for Catholics to gather and celebrate Holy Thursday's Mass.

GOOD FRIDAY'S liturgy is also a great blessing. The simplicity of the liturgy impresses upon us the significance of the suffering and death of Jesus. For many, Catholics, it is an emotional liturgy as it has the capacity to touch the human heart in a powerful way.

In addition to the liturgy of Good Friday, the devotion of the Stations of the Cross has become popular during Lent. Its origins lie in the customary pilgrimages that European Christians used to make to Jerusalem in early medieval times in order to walk the path that Jesus walked on his way to Calvary. When the Muslim takeover of the Holy Land made these trips too dangerous, Christians created a virtual walk back home eventually tagging the stopping points as "stations" for meditation and prayer. Over several centuries the number of "stations" varied from four to twenty, then in the mid eighteenth century Clement XII standardized the number at fourteen.

One of the reasons why the Stations of the Cross is a cherished devotion is its practical application to everyday life. Each station has its particular grace. For example, at the first station Jesus is condemned. Reflecting about this gives me the grace to deal with false accusation, whether I am the one falsely accused or, God forbid, the one doing the accusing. Over time, reflecting on this station tenderizes one's heart, making one more sensitive to the consequences of judging others and what we say about them. The second station gives us pause to reflect on our disappointments and failures with the grace to always get back up whenever we experience a fall. And so it goes, each station offering a grace to us as we walk with Jesus on His way to Calvary.

THE EASTER VIGIL completes the Triduum, the three day liturgical re-enactment of the Paschal Mystery of Jesus. All over the world on this night, the Church initiates its newest members through baptism, confirmation and first Eucharist. The impact of God's walk with the Jews in their covenant and with Christians in ours is proclaimed in the scriptures and brought to its conclusion in the celebration of Eucharist. It is the liturgy of liturgies. Don't miss it!

Dramatically presented and blessed at the Vigil is the Easter candle for the year. This candle represents the victory of Jesus over sin, suffering and death. It is Jesus who brings light and dispels the darkness. This candle remains visible in church throughout the year. There are two times when the Easter candle is lit for the individual Catholic, when we are baptized, and when we are buried. Both times the candle signifies a new birth, the first being born into the Body of Christ and becoming a child of God, and the second being born into eternal life, crossing over from the womb of this world to the new life with God in heaven.

Advent and Lent

Before Christmas and Easter, we Catholics get especially serious about our spiritual growth. During the four weeks of **ADVENT** we ponder the meaning of light in the darkness. Each week we light a candle to anticipate and celebrate the Light of the world that Jesus is. We try to appreciate how his teachings turn us into peacemakers, seekers of justice, and healers bringing forgiveness and reconciliation into troubled spots and much more.

During **LENT**, the six weeks before Easter, we get especially serious about our baptismal commitment to follow Jesus through the cross to eternal life. Again, the liturgy is our foundation. The daily readings on Sundays during Lent and weekdays as well touch every aspect of our lives. Since there is so much food for mind and heart a good way to grow spiritually is to look for "one piece of bread" one ray of light to shatter the darkness.

LESSONS FROM FRED AND ROSEMARY

For several years I was pastor of St. Frances Cabrini parish in Minneapolis. The congregation there taught me a lot about ministry to the dying. One month two well-known parishioners were dying. Fred Post had a condition that quarantined him in his final weeks. Not able to visit him, a cluster of parish members sang hymns and prayed for him from the hospital hallway outside his room. Fellow parishioners also supported his wife and children throughout the ordeal of his illness.

A short time after Fred's funeral celebration the parish secretary, Rosemary McGregor was terminally ill with cancer. Not having any family of her own, the parish was truly her family. One day I was asked by hospital staff to convince Rosemary that nothing more could be done for her in the hospital, and she needed to spend her last days at a nursing home. No way, she said and insisted that she be taken back to her apartment. "But there is no family to take care of you," I insisted. Then she said "Ask the people." The next Sunday we asked the congregation. For the next four weeks, people from the parish took care of her, 24/7, not only her physical needs but her spiritual as well.

Around noon on the day she died, I was called to come quickly because she seemed to be in her final moments. Not feeling well myself that day, I knew in my heart that Rosemary would not let go until I, her pastor, arrived, so I rested about an hour and then drove to her apartment. Surrounded by prayers and hymns, she welcomed me with her eyes, then closed them one last time as we prayed the last rites, and she passed peacefully into God's loving lap.

In those years, it had become popular for parishes to offer short courses on death and dying. No course could have taught more than what Cabrini parishioners learned from Fred and Rosemary.

About Death and Dying

Every Christian's experience of death and dying is unique to the individual and to family and loved ones surrounding that person. For many, death comes slowly or at least in such a way that he or she is comforted and lets go in a spirit of faith, hope and love. We should not be afraid to accompany a loved one in their last months, weeks, days or hours on this earth. Often miracles of grace happen to everyone involved. Prayers familiar to the dying person, the reception of the sacrament of Anointing of the Sick, favorite hymns, visit from friends and family—these things and more assist the dying person to let go and go home to God.

Growing in popularity nowadays is the idea of planning your own funeral even if it is likely to be years away. Some parishes have a staff member who assists those who choose to pre-plan their funeral. They choose the hymns, Scripture readings, pallbearers and lectors, homilist, presider, eulogist, and suggest other details, as much or as little as they wish.

In recent years many Catholics have chosen to be cremated. The Church has no objection to cremation, but recommends a preference for the traditional burial of the body. Even in the case of a cremation, our Church recommends that the body be visibly present for the visitation and funeral, with cremation and burial of the cremains to follow. The reason for this is the recognition that the grieving process happens more naturally when the body of the deceased is seen, good byes are expressed, and the death of the loved one is given finality. The ashes must be buried in a burial plot, rather than kept at home or strewn about. Again, the Church's wisdom favors the bereaved having a place to memorialize their beloved dead.

THIS ANCHOR OF EASTER PEOPLE WILL...

Ground you in the central Mystery of our faith, the Paschal Mystery, that is, the passion, death, and resurrection of Jesus.

Provide the best context for dealing with disappointment, illness, or failure.

Console you during the dying and loss of a loved one.

Bring joy to your heart as you appreciate, year after Liturgical Year, the great love God has for you.

CATHOLIC PRACTICE - SETTING THIS ANCHOR MORE FIRMLY...

Plan to participate in the Holy Thursday, Good Friday, and Easter Vigil services in your parish every year. Get it on your calendar now.

Become an active member of your parish community and worship with them every Sunday and Holy Day.

When a loved one dies, have a Mass offered for him or her and let the grieving family know that you are doing this in that person's memory.

Place priority on comforting those who are grieving: attend the wakes and funerals, send sympathy cards, offer to help whenever needed.

Receive the Sacrament of Reconciliation during Lent

Prepare a meal for a grieving family

ON BENDED KNEE... I pray for the faith to receive the Holy Spirit whom Jesus promised would remain with us as He took His place at the Father's right hand. Holy Spirit, empower me with a faith that holds me in your love, that opens my heart to love others, and pulls me toward greater hope and trust. Fill me with the Wisdom I need to live, daily, the Gospel of Jesus. Fill me with His commitment to be an instrument of peace and justice in the world. Fill me with His compassionate spirit and desire to serve. Amen.

ANCHOR NINE
Roman and Catholic

We are an apostolic Church, founded upon the twelve Apostles
and Saint Paul. We treasure the unity we enjoy with the
successors of Saint Peter and find ourselves gathered,
worldwide, around our local Bishops and their representatives.
We rest on the foundation of Jesus' words to Peter "Thou art
Peter and upon this rock I will build my Church."

In Communion with Rome

The word "catholic" means universal and the word "Roman" identifies the community of faith that traces itself to Saints Peter's and Paul's leadership of the Jesus movement. Tradition holds that Peter, the first Pope, and Paul, the great Evangelist, chose Rome as the center of their ministries. Both were buried in Rome, their grave sites honored over time by the construction of major places of worship. I remember the first time I visited the "Scavi", the excavations beneath St. Peter's basilica. As our tour group stepped lower and lower beneath St. Peter's basilica, following the path of recent archeological digs, I felt "goose bumps" when our guide informed us that we were approaching the level of the first century, and the actual burial place of the bones of St. Peter.

Was this the exact spot, I wondered? Having been previously in the Holy Land and visited Bethlehem where Jesus was born and Jerusalem where he died, I learned that "close" is close enough. The exact spot didn't matter. I was close enough. Christians living in Rome had kept Peter's grave in their collective memory, passing it on generation after generation. Churches had been built above Peter's grave more than once and then destroyed either by the ravages of time or unfriendly invaders. Today, St. Peter's basilica stands as a monument rising from medieval faith and genius. It, too, like monuments before, has meaning only in relation to the faith of its visitors. Many visitors come as tourists to be moved by its art and architecture. Others come as faithful pilgrims to be strengthened in their love of Christ and His Church.

Goose bumps came a second time when I visited the basilica of St. Paul's Outside the Walls. This church is honored as the burial place of St. Paul. Along its interior walls are ceramic images of all the popes from Peter to the present. The first time I saw these images I was struck by the long, continuous history of Roman Catholicism and the depth and richness of our historical collective memory. There they were for me, a student of history, bad popes along with the good. In the course of two millennia, our Church has survived failures and thrived with successes. Wasn't Judas one of the Twelve that Jesus Himself had chosen? Roman Catholicism has developed ways over its long history to embrace humanity's rough edges as well as its smooth.

What a difficult task it must be for our Pope and Bishops to keep us under one roof while at the same time nourishing the personal faith of a billion individuals. That is why we pray for our Pope and Bishops at every Mass! They have one huge responsibility and they appreciate our support for their leadership and service. Having traveled through some of Europe, Central and South America, and Kenya, I have seen a small part of the cultural differences that a global church like ours contains. It's awesome, to say the least. As a venerable pastor once told me: "'Tis a great Church that can hold us all!"

72

ONE BILLION BELIEVERS

Demographers say that we Catholics number about one billion believers worldwide. Imagine the challenge our Pope and bishops have to hold us all together in one community of faith. We are present in every nation and area of the globe. We represent hundreds if not thousands of cultures and sub-cultures, languages and dialects, customs and histories, rituals and philosophies. As American Catholics, we are enriched by the differences within our universal faith community, but we seem to be slow to recognize the wideness of our tent.

Some Contemporary Challanges

From the "get-go", the earliest beginnings of the Church, there were challenges confronting its leadership. Is the Gospel message of Jesus meant for Gentiles or only Jews? Must male gentile converts be circumcised? Whose leadership is the valid one when there are opposing claims? As Christianity expanded so did the number of challenges, and the ordained ministry of bishops, presbyters (priests) and deacons, along with the Faithful had to resolve them.

During the last 2,000 years, the Church has had to deal with many major issues, some were handled well, others not so well, but either way, the resolutions were steeped in the milieu of the times. The Crusades happened as a 200 year delayed response to the Muslim takeover of the Church's land and Holy Places in the East, and threatening to take over Western Europe as well. The Inquisition happened at a time when words were given more priority than human life itself, and statements judged by Church officials to be false were labeled as crimes against society. Church and state were too closely allied. These are just two examples from history.

Our own times present serious challenges as well. Our Bishops at the Second Vatican Council (1963-1965) set new directions for our Church's future, a few of which a half century later, are being re-interpreted. This should not come as a surprise, given the tensions built into humanity's attempts to touch the Divine.

LITURGY One area where this is happening is the Liturgy. For four hundred years before Vatican II, the celebration of Mass emphasized the transcendence of God, the Mystery of Jesus' Real Presence in the consecrated bread and wine, the dominance of males (priests and altar boys) as liturgical ministers, the effect of the Sacrament regardless of the people's active participation. Then, with the reforms of Vatican II, the "other dimensions were highlighted: the immanence of God, the Real Presence of God in the worshipping community, the rightful role of girls and women as liturgical ministers, and the active participation of the faithful in the Mass.

Vatican II also moved the Church from its post-Reformation stance of gazing upon itself to grazing confidently in the world. Developing harmonious relationships with other Christian churches and other world religions became a priority. The Council touched every aspect of Catholic life, giving it a new and exciting tone. Not all within the flock were excited, however, some feeling strongly that some changes stripped the Church of some of its treasures.

For my money, it is not a question of either/or but both/and. A simple illustration. My priest uncle purchased a St. Remy chalice, a chalice bedecked with precious jewels and gold, because of his emphasis on the Real Presence of Jesus in the consecrated Bread and Wine, a focus on transcendence, God's greatness and our call to worship, bowing our heads in reverent adoration. Following what I believed to be the "spirit of Vatican II" I began to use a clay chalice, investing not thousands but a mere few bucks, emphasizing God's immanence, the Divine presence in Jesus, born in the utter simplicity of a animal's manger. Is one right and the other wrong? Not to my thinking, but they surely are different, and they express what are, for many, opposing views.

Transcendence and immanence are both different dimensions of our Faith. But some other challenges are not. Celibacy for parish clergy is a matter of Church discipline, not a matter of belief. Few Catholics realize the fact that today, in Lebanon and Greece, for example, Catholic priests are not required to be celibate. My first exposure to this was when I served Mass in 1957 for a married Greek Catholic priest at the Catholic Youth Center boys camp. His wife was in the pews. He, as much a valid priest as any in the Western, Latin Church.

Also not a matter of faith are the customs and trappings from medieval times when triumphalism, clericalism and a male dominated leadership were the thing of the day. When I see or hear about some of these customs and trappings being revived I am disappointed. Some of our past is best encased in museums and left there. *Ecclesia reformanda*, the Church always in need of reform is one of our historical pieces of wisdom. So, every generation is called to live the Gospel more simply, more committed to serving beyond itself, more in touch with Jesus' call to service and a preferential option for the poor, and more profoundly intent on the active role of the laity, especially women, in all aspects of Catholicism. The "signs of the times' tell us that triumphalism and clericalism belong to our past!

ROLE OF WOMEN A serious complaint of some Catholic women is that ordination to priesthood is denied them. This fact alone is enough for some to write off the Church as their community of faith. I can empathize with these women and have been in touch with some of the pain this reality entails.

What is in our history? Certainly the Church's love and veneration of Mary, Jesus' mother, has had a positive effect for two millennia in Western civilization. Jesus treated women with openness, respect, acceptance and tenderness. He acted contrary to his culture's norms by speaking to women in public, by teaching, befriending, healing, and helping women the same as he would do to men. He respected their equality, reverenced their dignity, and invited them into his ministry. Women were part of his entourage and it was a woman, Mary Magdalene, who announced his Easter resurrection. There were deaconesses in the early Church and women played a prominent role in advancing the Gospel through their financial and moral support.

In the fifth century, when the Bishops of the Church gathered to refute those who were denying the divinity of Jesus (Council of Ephesus, 431) they declared that because of His divinity, Mary could rightly be called "Theotokos", Mother of God. We believe that Mary was graced by God and prepared for her role in salvation history from the moment of her conception. She accepted God's invitation to be the instrument by which God would take on our human nature. Thus, Mary is held in highest honor in the Church, not adored --only God is adored—but venerated. As Eve was the mother of the human race, so Mary is the New Eve, the Mother of redeemed humanity, and Mother of the Church..

Recorded history does not tell us much about the role of women in the first millenium but we do know about some women within the Church who held positions of authority and influence, Scholastica and Monica, for example. In Medieval times, women became abbesses of monasteries, having the same authority and role over monasteries of nuns (women) as abbots had over monasteries of monks (men). In fact, in 1115, an Abbess was in charge of a community of monks as well as a separate but related community of nuns. Perhaps the most well-known example of an Abbess ruling both monks and nuns is Saint Brigid of Kildare, having authority over just one of many similar arrangements among the Celtic monastic communities.

I grew up in an Italian sub-culture where women ruled the roost and the men were silently happy about it. But it was also a time in America when women did not receive equal pay for equal work, and had minimal opportunities to get a college education (which was true for the boys in my grade school class as well). Most boys went into the trades (carpentry, plumbing, management, etc.) and most girls into nursing, teaching, and homemaking. If a young woman wanted to get a college education, she had a good chance if she became a nun. For many young women in those days, a professional career (college president, college professor, even doctor of medicine) was possible if she joined the convent.

Today the role of women in Western societies has changed dramatically for the better. But such is not yet the case in many other parts of the world. That is why Pope John Paul II's Letter to Women was received in the Third World as a very liberal statement fostering feminism, while in the United States many received it as conservative and patriarchal. In the letter, John Paul called for equal opportunities for women in the professions, at all levels of education, and in every area of professional life and work.

> *"As far as personal rights are concerned, there is an urgent need to achieve real equality in every area: equal pay for equal work, protection for working mothers, fairness in career advancements, equality of spouses with regard to family rights and the recognition of everything that is part of the rights and duties of citizens in a democratic State."*
> Letter of Pope John Paul II to Women, page 13

We Catholics in North America do well to keep in mind the universal nature of our Church. Papal documents are written for the universal Church and are best read in light of that fact. While celebrating the advances made in our nation for justice and fairness to women, we realize that the work isn't finished, both within the Church and in society in general. But we can also celebrate the justice work being done under Catholic auspices in undeveloped countries as girls and young women are being educated in Catholic schools and encouraged to seek careers in the professions, and as women and men justice seekers keep the issue before the public.

CATHOLIC-UNIVERSAL-GLOBAL I can only imagine the challenges facing the Pope when he writes to Catholics worldwide about economic justice, morality, liturgical worship, and issues of wealth and poverty. Having spent a two month sabbatical in Rome in 1986, one thing I came to appreciate was the advantage the Pope has over other world leaders. His information channels are direct, and he can put his finger on the pulse not of one nation but of the entire globe. What other world leader is so informed?

A Lutheran minister pointed out to me years ago what he called "the genius of the Roman Catholic Church", namely, its simple and clean organizational structure. All parishes and most Catholic institutions are accountable to the local Bishop. Each Bishop, in turn, is accountable to the Pope. Of course, the Pope has help in this "chain of command" through relatively simple structures and instruments that keep Catholics united under one huge umbrella. It is remarkable. What makes it happen? Of course it doesn't happen without effort and without some deficiencies. No family or business or collection of people is perfect. But it is still remarkable how it all holds together.

There are **several keys to our unity:** commitment to Jesus and His teachings, commitment to His Church as we understand it and to its mission and purpose. Official documents of the Church, particularly the Code of Canon Law, the Catechism, the Sacred Liturgy and the doctrine of Apostolic Succession are major unifying factors that hold us together.

GLOBAL BUT REALIZED LOCALLY The local parish, where the mission of the Church is lived, is the heart of the Church worldwide. My most recent experience of parish life was as Pastor of St. Olaf parish in downtown Minneapolis. No two parishes are alike, and St. Olaf is like no other. At the time, we offered four Masses daily with eight on the weekends, confessions six days a week at sixteen different times often with two priests administering the sacrament, a social outreach program that included a food shelf, free store for clothing and furniture, and daily outreach to the homebound and elderly. Our educational programs included speakers on contemporary topics, a Faith and Work series for professionals, a marriage preparation program for the engaged, a young adult ministry, and faith formation programs for children, teens, and adults. A bookstore provided faith-related materials, and a cafeteria brought together downtown workers and parish members for food and conversation. Also, the church and chapel, open daily from 6 a.m. to 6 p.m., welcomed anyone and everyone to come in for prayer, meditation, or simply to enjoy some quiet time.

In 1992, St. Olaf parishioners dug deep and purchased an eight story residence next to the church as a partial answer to the city's homeless situation. Sub leased to Catholic Charities, the **EXODUS HOTEL** has been a temporary refuge to men and women living on the edges who, for one reason or another, needed an affordable room to rent while building up a rental history, and a safe place to stay on a temporary basis. The Exodus Hotel's capacity of 92 rooms has been filled consistently.

In addition to this outreach effort, St. Olaf parishioners also adopted **RISEN CHRIST** elementary school, an inner city school in South Minneapolis, providing the three hundred plus families there with much needed financial and volunteer assistance.Reaching beyond the Twin Cities to Africa, the parish was key in raising the funds necessary to build a high school in rural Kenya. All three of these relationships –the Exodus Hotel in downtown Minneapolis, Risen Christ

School in South Minneapolis, and **St. Timon's Secondary School in Kenya** continue to the present day.

None of this would have happened without the faithful and faith filled parishioners of this one parish. With thousands of parishes worldwide, we can be proud of the tremendous good being accomplished by Catholics who love their Church and want to help make good things happen everywhere. Parish life is "where it's at." That's where the faith is lived. Too often, the public's image of the Church is that of the central administration. As essential as the administrative arm is to the health of the whole Body, Bishops would be the first to tell you that "The parish is where it's at."

POLARIZATION The division of society into opposite extremes or opposing mind sets that refuse compromise, seems to be a characteristic of our time. When my generation was growing up, we put great stock in the common good. Perhaps because of the Great Depression, World War II and the ensuing Cold War, we felt we had to stick together if we were to survive. So, we didn't push the individuality button all that much. As did other Americans, American Catholics were willing to sacrifice selves for the good of the whole. Food was rationed, store shelves were relatively empty, money was scarce, air raid drills and bomb shelters were the common experience. We grew up with the conviction that we were all in this together so we were more than willing to put our personal interests further down our priority lists.

Then, in the late 1950's and 1960's, progress and affluence entered in, and the shift occurred away from the common good toward individuality. Our society seems better balanced now, but polarization is still prevalent.

In 1968, at the height of the turmoil of the infamous "Sixties" I had an experience that profoundly changed my life. I had been involved in the exciting movements for change, especially in our Church, because of the Second Vatican Council. Times were tense. Several of my friends in priesthood and religious Orders were leaving ministry, opposition to the Viet Nam War was gaining momentum, other movements and events were shaking up the status quo, notably Civil Rights, Feminism, Hippie Movement, Watergate, Gay rights, the sexual revolution, to name the most obvious.

I was working on a graduate degree at Notre Dame that summer, when the world seemed to be falling apart around me. Walking across campus one afternoon, feeling as depressed as I had ever felt, the memory of a childhood experience hit me like a ton of bricks. Thirty years earlier, when I was twelve, I visited my priest uncle in Texas. One day I watched him crush the head of a scorpion lying on his kitchen floor As he stepped on it with his shoe he told me to watch its tail. Then he said "When a scorpion is dying it kills itself off with its own poison." So I watched, and it did.

Why did that memory change me? In my enthusiasm to be a change agent, both in the Church and in society, I had become too negative in my preaching and teaching, overly critical of the "old ways". It was the recollection of the scorpion and my uncle's comment that told me that I (we) have the power to kill off any thing: family life, education, Church, religious communities, friendships, movements for justice and peace, you name it. And a poison that can kill all too effectively is a negative spirit. John, I said to myself, do you prefer to destroy good or to build it up? You have to choose: is it life or death, good or evil? You have one life to live and one life to give. What will it be?

So, I reaffirmed my love for my Church and I reaffirmed my vocational call to Baptism and to Priesthood. I had toyed earlier with the prospect of prophetic ministry, that is, to go radical! But prophets are often assassinated, can't always know for sure if their cause is truly right, are not guaranteed any followers, and besides, being a Prophet is tough work and a hard life. But the choice was mine, and I have never regretted it: serve the center, very widely so. Avoid the extremes. Strive to bring the polarized together, but do not take it personally if you fail. Polarization has a way of blinding its proponents and making your efforts useless, so, how much time do you want to waste? I chose to go with those who prefer moderation, are willing to make reasonable compromises, and can work together. It has been a great ride ever since!

Our Church is a noble institution. It has a divine mission to accomplish. To do so, it asks us to give our best to it, our most capable leaders to lead it, our most effective preachers to preach it, our most generous faithful to be the hands of Christ Jesus that serve the poor, teach the ignorant, visit the sick and imprisoned, and build up God's kingdom.

Institutions are to society and the social body what our critical systems are to our human body. Your body and mine are dependent on our blood systems, our nerve systems, our bone structures, our skin, to name the most obvious. If one system is sick, the whole body is affected. A physically healthy person has all the systems in good working order. So it is with our society, our social body. A well functioning government, an efficient and effective economic system, effective educational, religious, agricultural, and health-serving institutions –all these and more play their part in producing and maintaining a healthy society.

As we can't live well without healthy structures and systems in our physical bodies, so healthy societies need well-functioning institutions. To suggest that we can do without institutions is to bite the hand that feeds us. Individuals prosper well when the institutions prosper. There is no other way. We have an obligation to assure the health and well-being of our institutions.

The most recent warning sign that our Roman Catholic Church had better look into its institutional health was the revelation of sexual abuse of minors and children by priests. I make no excuse for this violation of religious vows and worse, the violation of innocent and vulnerable children. The fact that it has been approximately four per cent of clergy who have committed this crime, a small number, any number is an embarrassment to all Catholics. There may be explanations, not excuses, but even those pale in light of the tragedy of abuse. Added to this has been the failure of some bishops in the attempted cover-ups, thus failing to protect the young in their congregations and allowing the abusers to add more victims to their sin, sickness, and crime.

One of the disadvantages that institutions have, in general, is that they tend to change slowly. Thankfully, the U.S. Bishops, though far too slow in the beginning of the crisis, finally acted with decisiveness, thoroughness, and determination. A program was put in place that requires every Catholic parish and institution to do background checks on every one who works with children and youth. It also requires these personnel to attend training sessions and it requires that allegations of sexual abuse be reported immediately to proper civil authorities. **VIRTUS** is the program's title. As it is implemented, it will go a long way to restore at least some of the trust that Catholic clergy have lost as a result of this scandal.

One of the great scandals in Roman Catholic history is that of the "bad Popes", easily a very embarrassing fact to any member of the Church. But, at some point in my faith journey, I realized that it wasn't a failed Church I belonged to because of some dismal leaders, it was some "bad guys" who managed to get control of the Church. It can happen to any community of faith, especially one which is hierarchical and with enviable power and wealth. The wrong people, eager for financial gain and power, seem to find ways to work their way to the top. The miracle about such times is that, always in the midst of weak humanity, God's grace breaks out in new ways. Our worst times have produced some of our greatest saints.

The Church has weathered storms and scandals before, and has been strengthened in the aftermath. That is always the hope, and it is in the heart of what it means to be an Easter People. Good Fridays only last for a time, and are always followed by Easter Sundays.

After Jesus rose from the dead on that first Easter Sunday, He promised the gift of the Holy Spirit, a promise which He delivered on that first Pentecost Sunday. The experience the apostles and disciples had where they had gathered in fear and uncertainty was an overpowering thrust into the world to spread the Gospel (good news) about God's love for humanity, and God's invitation to everyone to embrace Jesus and His Gospel message of love.

The Presence of the Spirit was so profound that these early followers of Jesus began to experience some strange and wonderful gifts: the gift of prophecy, the gift of tongues, the gift of healing, and the gift of reconciliation.

Jesus had told them to go into the whole world and spread the good news of God's love and so they did. Not without difficulty, resistance, and even martyrdom did they spread out: the Apostle Thomas to places as far away as present day India, some of the others to Mesopotamia and beyond. Saul, later named Paul, one of the most effective persecutors of Jewish converts to the burgeoning Christianity, was literally knocked off his horse and within a year became the greatest Christian evangelizer ever. And the faithful followers of Jesus grew in numbers.

This Anchor of Roman and Catholic will...

Provide you with a "long view" of the Church's history and tradition, appreciating its role in shaping Western culture.

Provide you with a "wide view" of the Church's history and tradition, appreciating its current role in the world.

Provide a solid context for ecumenical dialogue and relationships (other Christian communities) and inter faith dialogue and relationships (Other world religions: Jewish, Muslim, Buddhist, Hindu and others).

Keep you grounded when discussing controversial and contemporary issues give you a balanced perspective on current happenings in Catholicism

Catholic Practice – setting this anchor more firmly...

Stay positive when discussing issues or differences about church leadership, parish life, directives from Rome and our local leadership. Maintain respect for both person and office.

Give feedback to church leaders in a responsible and kindly manner about suggestions you have or church-related problems you encounter. Encourage others to do the same.

Study Catholic history. Don't be satisfied with hearsay, but research topics of interest on your own and broaden your understanding of religious issues.

Subscribe to a Catholic magazine or journal, research its mission, its point of view.

Critique the saying "I am spiritual but not religious" from the perspective of the role of organized religion in spiritual development.

Research spiritualities within Catholicism, e.g. Franciscan, Benedictine, Ignatian, centering prayer, various forms of meditation, women's and men's spirituality.

On BENDED KNEE... Creator God, maker of human beings in Your own image. Guide Your Church as it sails the seas of our times. You are calling us to expand our horizons beyond those of earlier times. You have brought to our hearts through the insights of Vatican II the good that you have placed in other communities of faith. May your Spirit guide us in our efforts to understand our brothers and sisters who worship you in ways different from ours. Help us to know and love the identity You have given us in Jesus so that, grounded in our Christian faith, we may make progress in the building up of all peoples in justice and love. Amen.

ANCHOR TEN
Mary and the Saints

We have been blessed with a profound tradition of
reverence and relationship with Mary, the mother of Jesus,
as the first among the saints to receive Easter glory.
Full of grace from the moment of her conception,
Mary's role in salvation history is truly amazing grace.
She is not alone among those to be revered, however.
The whole Communion of Saints, all those who have gone
before us, marked with the sign of faith,
are one with us in Christ.

ALL SAINTS

My mother's mother, Nonna (Italian for Grandma) was as devout a Catholic as I have ever known. Her bedroom was like a shrine. It was dotted with statues of Jesus, Mary, Joseph and her special saint, Barbara. Nonna died when I was a young priest, and she was the first of my relatives at whose funeral I presided and preached. My father died a few months later, and I had his funeral, also. Over nearly a half century of priesthood, I have "buried" many other relatives and hundreds of others besides. As the years have passed, more and more I have come to appreciate the words of Jesus at the Last Supper, "This is my body, this is my blood, given for you." Isn't that what the Christian life is all about? Doing with our life what Jesus did with His?

Thirty-nine years after my dad died, I buried my mother. At the funeral I touched the casket bearing her spent body, and felt a profound sense of gratitude, for the thousands of meals she prepared, the dust and dirt she defeated, the prayers and counsel she dispensed, the countless ways she gave of herself for her family, her fellow parishioners, her friends, and her neighbors. "Grandma's cookies" remain a legend in our family. She lived the Mass, she lived the Eucharist, she echoed by her faith the meaning of the words of Jesus: This is my Body, my blood, my life, given for you! This is the stuff of which ordinary saints are made.

The Church celebrates ordinary saints on the *Feast of All Saints*, one of my favorite days because that day we remember and celebrate the everyday holiness and simple faith of all those holy ones who are not canonized. They remain an abiding blessing as we continue to walk our journey. Their faith inspires and encourages us as we strive to become Eucharist, bread for others.

Also inspiring and encouraging to us are the canonized saints, men and women officially recognized by the Church, and among whom the first is Mary, the Mother of Jesus.

MARY OF NAZARETH has been most highly revered throughout the entire life of the Church. Her role in salvation history is unique in that she was invited by God to become the instrument and vehicle by which God would take on our human nature and bring the Good News of God's love for humankind to the world.

Mary's role in the birth and life of Jesus is obviously central. She bore Him in her womb, delivered Him into the world, nursed and mothered him into adulthood. When He began his public ministry, she was there, along with other women and men, to watch the plan of God unfold. Mary saw how Jesus challenged the social norms of his time that denied equality to women and treated them as inferior to men. She watched Him as He broke the barrier which forbade men to speak to women in public. His miracles brought a little girl back to life, and cured women suffering from illnesses. When Mary asked Him to save a wedding party from embarrassment for running out of wine, He responded. Jesus' treatment of women was always with respect, tenderness, and equity.

Mary was front and center during Jesus' passion, crucifixion and death and she remained so as the followers of Jesus began to evangelize and spread the news about God's saving grace in Christ. The Apostle John took Mary into His care as she grew older, and as the Christian movement spread. Eventually Mary lived at Ephesus and it was there that she "fell asleep": this was her *dormition*, not death, since she was taken into heaven (Feast of the Assumption) as the first among the Holy Ones to receive the gift of Easter resurrection.

Over the centuries, Mary's place in salvation history has been reflected upon and named. She is seen as the New Eve. As Eve was the mother of the first creation of nature, Mary is the Mother of the new creation of Grace. As the early Church came to know Jesus as the Son of God, truly human and truly divine, Mary became revered as the Mother of God, *Theotokos*, in Greek. The revelation of who Jesus was and is unfolded over time and as it did, the profundity of Mary's role in salvation history became clearer.

It is no wonder that she has been and continues to be the most blessed of the saints. Worldwide, churches bear her name, communities of the faithful seek her protection, Catholics everywhere pray to God through her intercession. Devotion to her brings strength to mothers, solace to the suffering, hope to the despairing, and spiritual sustenance to all who call upon her. Mary is the first among all the saints to enjoy the fullness of grace and the fulfillment of God's promise of eternal life.

We Catholics love our saints. We have saints for just about everything: Saint Jude, helper with lost causes; Saint Anthony, finder of things lost; Saint Bernadine of Sienna, patroness of advertisers; Saint Helena, patroness of archeologists: Saint Thomas More, patron of attorneys; Saint Cecelia, patroness of composers; Saint Francis of Assisi, patron of environmentalists; Saint Anne, patroness of housekeepers; Saint Luke, patron of physicians; Saint Catherine of Siena, patroness of writers. The list is long. (Search Patron Saints of the Catholic Church for a more complete list.)

The Church's liturgical calendar highlights a wide variety of canonized saints, celebrating their feast days both at daily Mass and the Divine Office. Whenever I celebrate a saint's feast I always look for the grace, the unique aspect of that Saint's life, that is meant to inspire us that day. The Church's official Lectionary (the book of readings for Mass) gives us special scriptures that highlight the particular saint's life.

In addition to the liturgical schedule of readings for Mass, another source of liturgical prayer is the Divine Office, also called the *Liturgy of the Hours.* In the earliest centuries of the Church, especially after monasteries were founded, men and women who lived in these special communities developed a daily regimen of prayer and meditation. Over time it became standardized into sets of liturgical books built upon the Bible (both the Hebrew scriptures and the Christian scriptures) and the writings of Christian authors.

At its most developed stage, the Liturgy of the Hours divided the monastic day into seven segments, each of them being a time for the community members to gather for prayer. The first was around three a.m., followed by a morning prayer before Mass and breakfast, then the work day breaks for prayer at nine, noon, and three p.m.. Vespers was prayed around supper time and the final segment just before bedtime.

The Liturgy of the Hours remains a mainstay of religious communities today but has also become a regular part of the spirituality for lay persons. Available in simplified form with a subscription to www.giveusthisday.org, many Catholics worldwide follow the liturgical year praying the morning and evening formats it provides. It also has the readings and prayers for daily Mass for an even richer fare of spirituality.

When I was young, it was expected that every child born into a Catholic family would be given a saint's name. Among my generation, stories abound about certain pastors who insisted on a saint's name for every child they baptized. Some pastors bent a bit and allowed an exception, provided the child's middle name was a saint's. In recent times, lots of names not to be found among the list of saints are recorded in official church records, which means that future generations will have lots of new saints' names to choose from when the old custom of saints names rears back into vogue!

Another custom prevalent in my childhood was the wearing of a chain with a medal of one's patron or favorite saint. That custom, too, I expect to make a comeback. There is an inner peace that can accompany one's faith and trust in the Communion of Saints, that part of our faith that believes in their presence and potential in our daily lives.

We do not walk the Christian journey alone and unaccompanied. So gather your crew, choose your team. The Saints, after all, are still human. They love to be noticed and called upon.

This Anchor of Mary and the Saints will…

Provide you with the inner peace that comes with knowing that you do not walk the Christian life alone.

Provide inspiration in times of uncertainty, encouragement in times of weakness, and confidence in times of doubt.

Open your eyes to the wonders that God has worked in the lives of ordinary people and break open your heart in a spirit of gratitude.

Help you appreciate the feminine genius and the masculine genius embodied in God's plan for humankind.

Provide a source of grace and spiritual strength that is immediate and always there for you.

Catholic Practice – setting this anchor more firmly…

Know your patron saints, those whose names you may bear, those who represent your aspirations, your present or future occupations.

Become familiar with the saint(s) of your parish community.

Read a biography or more of American saints: Frances Cabrini, Kateri, Elizabeth Ann Seton, Katherine Drexler.

If you do not know how to pray the rosary, look it up, obtain one, and give it a try. It is a remarkable prayer form and one that provides an immediate link to the Communion of Saints, to Mary, and to the essential mysteries of our Faith.

On bended knee… God of great love. Thank You for the many ways You reveal Yourself to us, especially for the love manifested in Your saints, ordinary and exceptional. They are abiding gifts to us as we continue on our journeys of faith. Amen.

⚓ Anchors, Holding and at the Ready

It is truly a grace what God has done and continues to do through the Catholic faithful in spite of our human weaknesses. Over the centuries of growth and struggle, the Catholic Church has developed an exceptionally mature understanding of justice on both individual and social levels. It has produced saints, both recognized and not, who have given to humanity models of compassion and heroic virtue. The Catholic tradition is exemplary in its reverence for the mind, for nature, for human life, and for all creation. The Catholic Church has played a vital role in the development of Western Civilization, including the strengthening of democratic ideals and the formation of a just society.

Is there more work to be done? Surely. Are there challenges still to be met? Of course. Will the Church ever be perfect? Not this side of heaven! But our Church is a treasure worth cherishing, a community of faith worth belonging to, and a blessing not to be taken lightly or easily dismissed. Erasmus of Rotterdam, a humanist and critic of much of the Catholic culture of his time, was criticized by Martin Luther for remaining a Catholic. His response: "I put up with the Church in the hope that one day it will become better, just as it puts up with me in the hope that one day I will become better."

I believe that the ten anchors described in this book are gifts from God, and are important to cherish and promote if our lives are to be fulfilling, both for ourselves and for society at large. It is in our adolescent and young adult stages of life that we make many of the decisions that determine the strength and endurance of our anchors. Anchors have several uses. When the waters get rough we depend on them to keep us steady and safe in the storm. In times of calm and tranquility, just knowing the anchors are nearby and at the ready, is reassuring.

So, dear friend on the mighty seas, my prayer is that you will find these reflections helpful as you continue to navigate the Barque of Peter on your journey of faith. Let the Spirit of God fill your sails with winds of Wisdom and courage that you might know who you are as a child of God and a member of the Body of Christ.
My hope is that you have already or will begin soon to embrace your identity as a child of God, a member of the Mystical Body of Christ on this earth, while also recognizing the call now to become an active participant in the Catholic community of faith.

John E. Folit